Baptist Church Discipline

Baptist Church Discipline

A historical introduction to the practices of Baptist churches, with particular attention to the *Summary of Church Discipline* adopted in 1773 by the Charleston Baptist Association

James Leo Garrett, Jr.

REVISED EDITION

The Baptist Standard Bearer, Inc.
NUMBER ONE IRON OAKS DRIVE • PARIS, ARKANSAS 72855

Thou hast given a *standard* to them that fear thee;
that it may be displayed because of the truth.
-- *Psalm 60:4*

Revised Edition Printed by

THE BAPTIST STANDARD BEARER, INC.
No. 1 Iron Oaks Drive
Paris, Arkansas 72855
(479) 963-3831

The WALDENSIAN EMBLEM
lux lucet in tenebris
"The Light Shineth in the Darkness"

First Edition Copyright 1962
Broadman Press, Nashville, TN
Reprinted by permission   ISBN #1-57978-352-X

PREFACE TO THE SECOND EDITION

More than a third of a century — in fact 42 years — has transpired since Baptist Church Discipline was published by Broadman Press, and for much of that period this booklet has been out of print. The original edition had two objectives: to make available, for the first time in more than a century, a published text of the 1774 Charleston (S.C.) Baptist A Summary of Church Dicipline [sic], and to focus attention on the issue of church discipline, both its abandonment and its recovery, in the early 1960s.

These intervening years have witnessed Vatican Council II, the Civil Rights Movement, social unrest and rejection of traditional values, the Vietnam War, the breakup of the USSR and the end of the "Cold War," radical changes in sexual morality and family life, and the advent of revolutionary new technology. American Protestantism has become more polarized into two major camps: the "mainline" or ecumenical churches and the "evangelical" churches. The Southern Baptist Convention has been engaged in divisive internal controversy for the last twenty-five years. African-American Baptists have experienced two schisms resulting in the formation of two new national conventions. Baptists in the Two-Thirds World, many of whom practice a stricter church discipline than Baptists in the United States, have become more numerous, there now being five nations — India, Brazil, Nigeria, Democratic Republic of Congo, and South Korea — with more than half a million Baptist church members.

Concurrently there have been significant studies of Baptist church discipline even though there is little evidence of a renascence of the intentional and consistent practice of any congregational discipline, apart from the discipling of new Christians, in churches related to the larger Baptist conventions in the United States.

Writing for American Baptists, Norman Hill Maring and Winthrop Still Hudson in their 1963 manual stated succinctly that "exclusion" was a "practice" that "has virtually disappeared from our churches." Asserting, however, that "there are times when persons should be excluded from the fellowship," these authors put the stress on "indifferent" and "<u>inactive members,</u>" with no mention of heresy, immorality, or divisiveness.[1] But in their 1991 revision of the same manual Maring and Hudson identified termination of church membership "because of scandalous behavior, teachings which embarrass the church of Christ, or failure to live up to covenant obligations" and then delineated a separate procedure for placement of inactive members on an "<u>inactive membership list.</u>"[2]

James Willard Bartley, Jr., in his study in the Pauline epistles, differentiated the texts which deal with corrective discipline for "social and moral problems" — "disorderly conduct" (1 Thessalonians 2:11-12; 4:11-12; 5:14; 2 Thessalonians 3:6-15) and "extreme sexual immorality" (1 Corinthians 5:1-13) from the texts relative to "doctrinal problems" — "heretical preachers" (Galatians 1:6-9; 6:1), "divisive elements" (Romans 16:17-20), and "drifting from sound doctrine" (1 Timothy 1:18-20; 5:19-20; 6:3-5; 2 Timothy 4:14; Titus 1:9-16; 3:10).[3]

Charles William Deweese, quoting Findley B. Edge, Norman H. Maring/Winthrop S. Hudson, and J. Herbert Gilmore, Jr., noted in 1978 indications of a possible recovery among Baptists of congregational discipline that was "reformative" as well as "formative." His own review of the biblical materials included the Old Testament and the Dead Sea Scrolls. Baptists ought not to bypass the numerous biblical passages but should combine "discipline and forgiveness." In his survey of the earlier Baptist

---

[1] <u>A Baptist Manual of Polity and Practice</u> (Valley Forge, PA: Judson Press, 1963), p. 80.

[2] Ibid., rev. ed., 1991, p. 84.

[3] "Corrective Discipline in the Pauline Epistles," Th.M. thesis, Southwestern Baptist Theological Seminary, 1965

PREFACE TO SECOND EDITION

practice Deweese noted that "Baptist church discipline has been a natural corollary of church covenants" and that the demise of discipline was at least partly "a reaction to the legalistic use of discipline and covenants" devoid of serious efforts towards reclamation and restoration. He offered nine suggestions for contemporary application.[4]

J. Ernest Runions of Canada identified "three major New Testament passages" that bring together discipline and the church: Matthew 16:13-20; 18:15-20; Revelation 2, 3. "Two other passages illustrate the apostolic implementation of discipline": 1 Corinthians 5:1-13 and 2 Thessalonians 3:6-16. "Taken together," these groups of texts "link the themes of covenant, holiness and the reign of God in Christ."[5] He interpreted the binding and loosing in Matthew 16:19 as referring to excommunication and found in Matthew 18:15-20 "a disciplinary sequence which is at once the action of the church and of Christ." Revelation 2,3 demonstrates Christ's method of discipline by entreaty and exhortation and by chastisement and restoration after repentance. The Pauline texts reveal "the depth of christological authority committed to the Church." Paul commands because "he is himself under the Word of Christ." "The gathered church will make a decision that is the apostle's decision. But the apostle acts for Christ, so the decision will be Christ's decision."[6] The "first step" in church discipline (Matthew 18:15) "is to be private," the emphasis is to be on restoration, and ecclesial discussion "should be used only as a last resort when other attempts have failed." The "anathema" was seemingly used only "for those who blasphemously rejected the gospel of grace and the finality

---

[4] A Community of Believers: Making Church Membership More Meaningful (Valley Forge, PA: Judson Press, 1978), 63-80.

[5] "Discipline and Discernment," in The Believers' Church in Canada: Addresses and Papers from the Study Conference in Winnipeg, May 15-18, 1978, ed. Jarold K. Zeman and Walter Klaasen (Brantford, Ont.: Baptist Federation of Canada; Winnipeg, Man.: Mennonite Central Committee, 1979), p. 120.

[6] Ibid., pp. 120-22.

and authority of Jesus Christ" (Galatians 1:8; 1 Corinthians 16:22). "Both the Reformers and the Believers' Churches recognized the authoritative nature of church discipline and ... that it must be the action of the whole people of God in a given place." Runions, acknowledging that abuses have led to the demise of post-baptismal corrective discipline, insisted that restoration of offenders is of higher priority than "moral purity in the church and orthodoxy of church doctrine."[7]

Stephen Michael Haines in a 1984 dissertation studied the practice of church discipline in fifteen selected Southern Baptist churches, both rural and urban, located in ten states during the period from 1880 to 1939.[8] He identified six basic causes of the demise of church discipline among Southern Baptists: "the secularization of American society, the rise of individualism both in the culture and among Baptists, with a consequent loss of community values, the legalistic and punitive character of the earlier practice of corrective discipline, a more optimistic view respecting human beings and sin, the adoption by the churches of efficiency and quantification of goals from the business world, and the silence about or the opposition to church discipline in denominational publications."[9]

Don Baker, senior pastor of Hinson Memorial Baptist Church, Portland, Oregon, narrated his congregation's 26-month experience in corrective discipline of a ministerial staff member who was found to have had adulterous relations with ten women during thirteen years, who confessed his sin and whose wife forgave him and stayed with him, with the church's withdrawing his ordination and insisting that he remain in its membership and under its care, and who, after a year of

---

[7] Ibid., pp. 122-26.

[8] "Church Discipline as Practiced by Representative Southern Baptist Churches, 1880-1939," Ph.D. diss., Southwestern Baptist Theological Seminary.

[9] Ibid., 178-99, as summarized by the present author in his Systematic Theology: Biblical, Historical, and Evangelical, vol. 2, 2d ed. (North Richland Hills, TX: BIBAL Press, 2001), p. 601.

psychological counseling, was reordained and subsequently called to the pastorate of another church.[10]

J. Carl Laney wrote a full-length monograph on church discipline out of the conviction that the churches in the United States are "infected" with a weakening "moral blight" and that such infection "is due, at least in part, to a neglect of church discipline." He defined church discipline in two ways: as "<u>God's loving plan for restoring sinning saints</u>" and as "<u>the confrontive and corrective measures taken by an individual, church leaders, or the congregation regarding a matter of sin in the life of a believer</u>." It is to be primarily restorative, not punitive.[11] Neglected in Corinth and in Thyatira and related to the sin of Achan (Joshua 7), church discipline finds its pattern in Hebrews 12:4-13. After noting roadblocks to initiating such discipline and sketching the history of church discipline, Laney listed four types of sin that may require discipline: "<u>violations of Christian love</u> ["private offenses"], <u>unity</u> [divisiveness], <u>law</u> [immorality], <u>and truth</u> [heresy]"[12] After expounding the teaching of Jesus in Matthew 18:15-17 and the teaching of Paul, he found authority in the keys and restoration as the great purpose. The results when church discipline succeeds and those when it fails were identified, and special attention was given to the discipline of church leaders and to the danger of civil lawsuits.[13] Laney concluded with a report of his 1984 survey of Protestant pastors (439 responses out of 1,250), in which 51 percent of the cases were said to have led to restoration, and transfer of membership to another church to be a deterrent to

---

[10] <u>Beyond Forgiveness: The Healing Touch of Church Discipline</u> (Portland, OR: Multnomah Press, 1984).

[11] <u>A Guide to Church Discipline</u> (Minneapolis: Bethany House Publishers, 1985), pp. 12-14.

[12] Ibid., pp. 18-47.

[13] Ibid., pp. 48-139. Especially the 1984 case of Marian Guinn and the Collinsville, OK, Church of Christ.

effective church discipline, and with eighteen crucial questions respecting church discipline.[14]

In a British context David Coffey affirmed that "the discipline of believers" is "emphasized" in the Bible, "has always been the practice of the church," and "is the church exercising its divine authority." When authority smothers freedom, authoritarianism will likely result, but when freedom reigns over authority, there will likely follow that individualism in which "the biblical doctrine of 'the priesthood of all believers' has been distorted into 'the papacy of each believer.'" Although there surely have been abuses, church discipline is intended to preserve "the purity of the church," protect "the reputation of the church," prevent "the erosion of moral standards," and restore "the offender to full fellowship." Discipline is needed when there is "a threat to the unity of a fellowship," "to the truth of the gospel," or to "the moral beauty of the fellowship." We are to preach the word of God in love "to censure those who are careless," to "excommunicate the impenitent" with a view to restoration, and to make and live out the church covenant.[15]

In his 1987 article George B. Davis first elaborated on seven reasons for the modern neglect of church discipline: the "denial of the biblical mandate" (Matthew 18:15-18), church discipline as unrealistic since perfection is not attainable, "the wrong interpretation of some passages of Scripture" (Matthew 7:1-6; 13:24-30, 36-43, 47-50), past abuses of church discipline, the appearance of discipline as being marked by "an unloving spirit," the lack of present-day models, and practical difficulties in its implementation.[16] Then Davis argued for the "necessity" of church discipline by articulating seven objectives of church discipline: the glorifying and honoring of God by holiness and

---

[14] Ibid., pp. 139-63.

[15] Build That Bridge (Eastbourne, U.K.: Kingsway Publications, 1986), pp. 103-26. Coffey's chapter is entitled "Discipline Is Discipleship."

[16] "Whatever Happened to Church Discipline?" Criswell Theological Review 1 (Spring 1987): 345-52.

obedience, the reclamation of "the wayward member," the protection of the remainder of the church from heresy, immorality, or divisiveness, the maintenance of the church's reputation, the deterring of others from sin, the preventing of judgment by God, and helping to "maintain a regenerate church membership."[17]

Writing in the United Kingdom, Michael John Collis gave detailed attention to the history of Baptist church discipline. First, the biblical materials, including the Dead Sea Scrolls and the Didache, were reviewed. Second, the English Baptist doctrine of the church was traced, primarily through early confessions of faith and recent monographs. Third, what was identified as the "theology of church discipline amongst Baptists" was actually a treatment of the views of John Calvin, of John Owen, and of the Baptist, Andrew Fuller. Fourth, the English Baptist practice of church discipline was traced historically. Fifth, the import for church discipline of English Baptist church covenants was explored. Sixth, Collis treated the contemporary practice of discipline among Baptists in the United Kingdom on three levels: (1) "the local church,"[18] (2) the association,[19] and (3) the Baptist Union of Great Britain.[20] Finally he offered suggestions for contemporary renewal of church discipline.[21]

John William MacGorman addressed the issue of contemporary church discipline by means of an exegesis of 1 Corinthians 5:1-13, from which he drew five conclusions: discipline in this case

---

[17] Ibid., pp. 352-61.

[18] Including cases involving Freemasonry.

[19] Including the case of Jesus Fellowship Church (Baptist) and the Northamptonshire Baptist Association.

[20] Including the discipline of ordained ministers, the theology of Michael Taylor, and the removal from membership in the Baptist Union of Jesus Fellowship Church.

[21] "The Theology and Practice of Church Discipline amongst Baptists with Particular Reference to Baptists in the United Kingdom," Th.M. thesis, Heythrop College, University of London, July 1988.

"was not exercised over trivialities" (rather over incest), "was exercised by the whole church," "was redemptive rather than punitive," "was realistic about the contagiousness of evil," and "generally called for exclusion from the church." In conclusion he listed six reasons for the contemporary failure to practice corrective church discipline.[22]

Wayne Grudem in his systematic theology, after treating "the purity and unity of the church" and prior to his lengthy chapter on "church government," dealt with "the power of the church." After asserting the reality of spiritual warfare, interpreting binding and loosing in both Matthew 18:18 and 16:19 as referring to church discipline, and arguing that church discipline should be exercised by the church and not by civil government, Grudem explicated three purposes of corrective church discipline: "restoration and reconciliation" of the straying believer, keeping "the sin from spreading to others," and protecting "the purity of the church and the honor of Christ."[23]

The present author in his systematic theology treated "excommunication of members" in a chapter pertaining to "membership of churches." The Old Testament, the Dead Sea Scrolls, and the Babylonian Talmud were explored for pertinent teaching and practice, and the New Testament materials were reviewed. Under the postbiblical history major attention was given to Anabaptists and to Baptists, and the contemporary problem was only briefly treated.[24]

In his revision of Edward T. Hiscox's nineteenth-century manual, Everett C. Goodwin noted that "exclusion" from church membership may occur "for several reasons, but never

---

[22] "The Discipline of the Church," in The People of God: Essays on the Believers' Church ed. Paul A. Basden and David S. Dockery (Nashville: Broadman Press, 1991), pp. 74-84.

[23] Systematic Theology: An Introduction to Biblical Doctrine (Leicester, U.K.: Inter-Varsity Press; Grand Rapids: Zondervan Publishing House, 1994), pp. 887-903.

[24] Garrett, Systematic Theology: Biblical, Historical, and Evangelical, 2:596-602.

without reflection and prayer. Most often it would follow the determination of the church that the member was not worthy to continue in relationship because of failure to exercise appropriate membership responsibilities or because the life of the person indicated a consistent manner of living in defiance of the spirit of the gospel."[25] Goodwin retained some of Hiscox's extensive treatment of church discipline, including the "Three Laws of Christ's House" ("for every disciple, the law of love"; "for the offender, the law of confession"; and "for the offended, the law of forgiveness"), procedures for dealing with "private offenses" and with "public offenses," and positive church discipline (or discipleship).[26]

Gregory A. Wills has produced an intensive, well-researched study of the practice of corrective church discipline by and among Baptist churches in Georgia between 1785 and 1900 and its demise by the early twentieth century. Wills delineated the use of the Saturday church conference and discipline committees, the adherence to Matthew 18:15-17, church trials that involved either voluntary confession or properly authorized accusation, the goal of repentance, forgiveness, and restoration, and the application to women and to Negro slaves and later freedmen and in independent Negro churches. Wills contended that this democratically administered Baptist church discipline was antithetical to that individualism and quest for freedom that would allow individual Baptists to determine their own beliefs and set their own moral standards apart from the congregation.[27]

At the beginning of the twenty-first century and the new millennium Baptist churches face awesome challenges, not the

---

[25] The New Hiscox Guide for Baptist Churches (Valley Forge, PA: Judson Press, 1995), p. 44.

[26] Ibid., pp. 195-205.

[27] Democratic Religion: Freedom, Authority, and Church Discipline in the Baptist South, 1785-1900 (New York: Oxford University Press, 1997). No attempt has been made to include in this survey numerous D.Min. theses which relate to church discipline in specific Baptist congregations.

least of which is the integrity of their own memberships. I am grateful to Pastor Bill W. Lee and Baptist Standard Bearer, Inc., for authorizing and publishing this new edition of <u>Baptist Church Discipline</u>.

                                    James Leo Garrett, Jr.
                                    Southwestern Baptist Theological Seminary
                                    February 2004

PREFACE TO THE FIRST EDITION

The Charleston Baptist "*Summary of Church Discipline*" is the oldest document pertaining to church discipline framed by Baptists in the South. Yet for more than a century there has been no reprint of this document. Not only have several generations of Baptist pastors and laymen been unfamiliar with it but also until the recent advent of microfilm it has been relatively inaccessible to those who would subject it to scholarly investigation.

The editor wishes to express gratitude for helpful counsel and assistance from the following: Rev. H. Claude Simmons, Fort Worth, Texas, in whose company and with whose cooperation the idea for this edition was conceived; Drs. W. J. Fallis and J. F. Green, Jr., of Broadman Press; Dr. Leo T. Crismon, Miss Betty McCoy, Mrs. Ronald Deering, Dr. Clayton Sullivan, and the staff of Boyce Centennial Library, Southern Baptist Theological Seminary, Louisville, Kentucky; Rev. and Mrs. W. David May, Bloomington, Indiana; his colleagues of the faculty of Southern Baptist Theological Seminary, especially Drs. Henlee H. Barnette, Findley B. Edge, Dale Moody, E. C. Rust, E. J. Vardaman, and Wayne E. Ward; Dr. W. L. Lumpkin, Norfolk, Virginia; the editorial board of the *Southwestern Journal of Theology* for permission for quotation, and Drs. Robert A. Baker and W. P. Greenlee, Southwestern Baptist Theological Seminary, Fort Worth; Dr. Davis C. Woolley, executive-secretary, the Historical Commission of the Southern Baptist Convention, and Miss Helen Conger, librarian, Dargan Carver Library, Nashville, Tennessee; Rev. Glendon Grober, Rev. Aubrey Leon Morris, Rev. Harold Wahking, Dr. John R. Claypool, and Mr. Wayne O. Craig, Louisville; Dr. Sam S. Hill, Jr., Chapel Hill, North Carolina; Rev. W. C. Smith, Raleigh, North Carolina; Mrs. E. Glenn Hinson, efficient typist of the manuscript; Mrs. Dennis Kissinger and Mrs. Jimmie W. Capel;

and his wife whose unfailing patience and encouragement are hereby acknowledged.

JAMES LEO GARRETT, JR.

TABLE OF CONTENTS

1. Preface to the Second Edition .... Page i

2. Preface to the First Edition .... Page xi

3. Introduction .... Page 1

4. Text of the Charleston Discipline .... Page 29

    Of a True and Orderly Gospel Church .... Page 34

    Of Church Officers .... Page 37

    Of Receiving Persons to Church Membership .... Page 41

    Of the Duties Incumbent on Church Members .... Page 46

    Of Church Censures .... Page 49

    Of the Associations of Churches .... Page 57

5. Biography and Picture of the Author .... Page 63

INTRODUCTION

Baptists in the United States, and Southern Baptists in particular, are giving meager evidence of having today an ordered, disciplined churchmanship. This appears to be true whether one considers ethics, theology, or church order. Moral failures, which often are crimes as well as sins, increasingly occur among church members — Baptists and otherwise — and are reported in the public press. Even ordained ministers and other church leaders may experience such failures and no action by the congregation or by denominational bodies be taken. Many church members seem quite insensitive to the religious and moral dimensions of contemporary social issues such as race relations, church and state, war and peace.

Despite some indications of a renewed theological concern there is among Baptists widespread indifference toward the great Christian affirmations. While claiming to revere the Bible and to adhere to the New Testament as the basis of religious authority, Southern Baptists have been too little involved in the renewal of biblical theology.

The inroad of secularism and materialism into Baptist lives and Baptist churches is more real than acknowledged. Inactive and nonparticipating church members and the problem of nonresident membership have become major Southern Baptist difficulties.[28] The increasing number of Baptist church members seeking "rebaptism" on the basis of having been converted to Christ after initial "baptism" in Baptist churches is largely a twentieth-century phenomenon. Friction between

---

[28] Allen W. Graves, "How Can We Prevent the Non-Resident Problem?" *Baptist Messenger*, XLI (March 6, 1952), 9; "How Can We Solve the Non-Resident Problem?" *ibid.*, XLI (Feb. 21, 1952), 11; Charles F. Leek, "Nonresident Church Members," *Encyclopedia of Southern Baptists* (Nashville: Broadman Press, 1958), II, 981f.; Ralph H. Langley, "Move Those Letters," *The Baptist Program* (Jan., 1961), p. 7.

pastor and deacons, pastor and congregation, pastor and church staff, and deacons and congregation abounds and sometimes erupts into major congregational schisms.

Southern Baptists are affording some leadership and example in the fields of evangelism, religious education, church administration, religious radio and television, and pastoral care. Yet, in the practice of an ordered, disciplined congregational life — that which Littell calls the central concern of the "free church" tradition in its beginnings[29] — Southern Baptists are providing neither leadership nor example.[30]

Nevertheless, a slowly growing awareness of the need for some kind of renewal of personal and congregational spiritual discipline among Southern Baptists is in evidence. "Voices from within the Southern Baptist Convention increasingly are raised in diagnosis of the malady of Southern Baptist churchmanship which is contemporaneous with the mild vitality" of the post-World War II "Southern Baptist advance."[31]

---

[29] Franklin H. Littell, *The Free Church* (Boston: Starr King Press, 1957), p. 1. Littell affirms that the free church tradition centers in the committed, disciplined church more than in the church's separation from the state.

[30] Cf. James Leo Garrett, "Seeking a Regenerate Church Membership," *Southwestern Journal of Theology*, III (April, 1961), 25.

[31] *Ibid.* Cf. L. C. Craig, "Maintaining Church Discipline," *Baptist Standard*, LXI (June 30, 1949), 6; H. W. Schafer, "Church Discipline: a Lost Doctrine," *Western Recorder*, CXXIV (February 9, 1950), 9, 25; Max Stanfield, "Church Disturbers," *Baptist Messenger*, XL (April 19, 1951), 5; L.C. Quarles "Church Discipline and Infallibility," *Religious Herald*, CXXIV (August 10, 1951), 4; "Leaving Off the Varnish," *Baptist New Mexican*, XL (March 27, 1952), 1; J. Edgar Mobley, "Church Discipline Needed," *Baptist Courier*, LXXXIV (October 30, 1952), 8; Morgan Kizer, "More About Discipline," *Baptist Courier*, LXXXIV (November 20, 1952), 9; Carl Loy, "Church Discipline," *Western Recorder*, CXXVII (September 24, 1953), 5, 8; W. C. Taylor, "Church Discipline," *Western Recorder*, CXXVII (October 8, 1953), 5; J. W. MacGorman, "A Vanishing Baptist Distinctive," *Christian Index*, CXXXVI (July 18, 1957), 6; Theron D. Price, "Discipline in the Church," in Duke K. McCall, ed., *What Is the Church?* (Nashville: Broadman Press, 1958), pp. 164-85; Erwin L. McDonald, "Revival of Church Discipline?" *Arkansas Baptist*, LVIII (July 16, 1959), 4; James Leo Garrett, "Church Discipline: Lost, But Recoverable," *Western*

INTRODUCTION 3

Prior to an examination of the Charleston *Summary of Church Discipline* itself, it is fitting that inquiry be made concerning the history of church discipline.

The Old Testament records instances of divinely ordained acts of discipline within the community of Israel, sometimes by divine intervention through nature, as in the Korah-Dathan-Abiram rebellion (Numbers 16, esp. vv. 31-35) and in the Nadab-Abihu incident (Leviticus 10:1 ff.), and sometimes through human instrumentality, as in the idolatry of the golden calf or bull (Exodus 32, esp. vv. 25- 29,35). The law prohibited or delayed admission to the assembly of Israel of those who had committed certain sexual offenses or were from among Israel's enemies (Deuteronomy 23:1-8). Specific instruction in the law (Deuteronomy 6:1-9) and the rediscovery and public reading of the law (Joshua 8:34f.; 2 Kings 23:1-3), as well as the many exhortations of Israel's leaders, were indicative of positive discipline. Failure to attend promptly Ezra's reform assembly, thus subjecting the offender to forfeiture of all his property and separation "from the assembly of the captivity," is an example of postexilic discipline designed to effect separation from foreign wives (Ezra 9:1 ff.; 10, esp. v. 8, ASV).

The Babylonian Talmud contains references to the practice of the *shammetha* or ban with three degrees in Judaism. First, there was a "reprimand" (*neziphah*) for a period of seven days. This was to be followed by a "separation" or exclusion (*niddui*), which in Babylon lasted for seven more days but in Palestine for thirty days. A third and most decisive action was "full excommunication" (*cherem*) of indefinite duration.[32] There is

---

Recorder, CXXXIII (July 23, 1959), 3f.; Bill G. West, "Where Do Southern Baptists Stand with Reference to Church Discipline?" *Baptist Standard*, LXXII (January 6, 1960), 10f.; Bill G. West, "Front Door Discipline," *The Baptist Program* (January, 1961), 22; Charles Chaney, "A Case for Backdoor Discipline," *The Baptist Program* (September, 1961), p. 3.

[32] Mo'ed Katan 14*b*, 15*a*, 15*b*, 16*a*, 16*b*, 17*a*, *The Babylonian Talmud*, Seder Mo'ed, trans. and ed. by I. Epstein (London: Soncino Press, 1938), Megillah, VIII, 85-109; cf. fn. 5, p. 90; fn. 12, pp. 97f. The power of excommunication was exercised by the

also evidence of Judaism's recognition of three cardinal sins (heathenism, incest and related acts, and homicide).[33] The Jewish practice of excommunication serves to clarify the reluctance of the parents of the man blind from birth whom Jesus healed to precipitate their excommunication from the synagogue (John 9:22).[34]

The discovery of the Dead Sea Scrolls has revealed the nature of the discipline within the Qumran community. Initiation into the community was conditioned upon a covenant or pledge and included a rehearsal by priests of "the bounteous acts of God" toward Israel and one by Levites of the iniquities of Israel.[35] An initiate was examined "concerning his temper in human relations and his understanding and performance in matters of doctrine" and thereby was assigned to a rank within the community.[36] Those were to be excluded from the community for life who cursed God, who slandered or complained against the community, and who, after at least ten years within the community, lapsed.[37] One passage in the *Manual of Discipline* is similar to Matthew 18:15f.[38]

---

high court at Jamnia. Cf. George Foot Moore, *Judaism in the First Centuries of the Christian Era* (Cambridge, Mass.: Harvard University Press, 1927), II, 183. A prayer for "the extirpation of heretics," including "Nazarenes" or Jewish Christians, was introduced in the time of Gamaliel II, *ibid.*, I, 292; III, 97, n. 68.

[33] Moore, *op. cit.*, II, 58, 267.

[34] Cf. Alfred Edersheim, *The Life and Times of Jesus the Messiah* (Grand Rapids: Wm. B. Eerdmans Publishing Co., 1953), II, 183f.

[35] *Manual of Discipline* 1:1 to 2:18, in *The Dead Sea Scriptures*, trans. and ed. by Theodor H. Gaster (Garden City, N.Y.: Doubleday and Co., 1956).

[36] *Ibid.*, 5:20-24, as trans. by Gaster.

[37] *Ibid.*, 6:27; 7:16f., 22-25.

[38] *Ibid.*, 5:26 to 6:1. Cf. W. H. Brownlee, trans. *The Dead Sea Manual of Discipline* (Bulletin of the American Schools of Oriental Research, Supplemental Studies, 10-12, 1951), p. 23, fn. 3. There is evidence that Essene discipline went to extremes, involving death or near death because of adherence to Essene food regulations by those expelled. Cf. *Zadokite Fragment*, ed. by Chaim Rabin (Oxford: Clarendon Press, 1954), p. ix, 17-x, 2; Josephus, *Wars of the Jews*, II, 8f., cited by Jerry

INTRODUCTION

In the New Testament there is a significant, though not too obvious, connection between discipline and discipleship. Particularly is this manifested in the Gospels. The word "discipline," which is derived from the Latin *disciplina,* and the word "discipleship," derived from the Latin *discipulus,* have a common rootage in the Latin verb *discere,* "to learn."[39] The teaching of Jesus about discipleship had a direct bearing upon the order and ethics of the New Testament churches, and likewise any contemporary renewal of congregational discipline should be consistent with the nature of Christian discipleship.

Christian discipleship, according to the teaching of Jesus, is denial of one's self and taking of one's cross (Mark 8:34), taking the yoke of Jesus (Matthew 11:28-30), and becoming as little children (Matthew 18:3). Christians are to be "the salt of the earth" and "the light of the world" (Matthew 5:13-15). They are those who "hunger and thirst after righteousness" and whose righteousness exceeds that of the scribes and Pharisees (Matthew 5:6,20). Like a wise tower builder or prudent king about to go to war, one should reckon the cost of discipleship, for a disciple's relation to Jesus is to his relation to his family as love is to hate (Luke 14:25-33). Discipleship is marked by love of one's fellow disciples (John 15:12-13) and by hatred by the world (John 15:17-20), for the disciples of Jesus are "not of the world" yet are sent "into the world" (John 17:14,18). Greatness in discipleship is measured by ministering servanthood (Mark 10:43f.), and being a disciple of Jesus means involvement in the making and teaching of other disciples (Mark 1:17; Matthew 28:19f.).

The Gospels also give evidence of failure in discipleship. Since its design is fruit-bearing, detachment from Jesus the vine (John

---

Vardaman, "Significant Developments in Scroll Research," *Review and Expositor,* LXIII (Apr., 1961), 199.

[39] *Discipuli* is the Vulgate rendering of *mathetai* the Greek New Testament word for "disciples," while *disciplina is* used in the Vulgate, for example, to translate *paideia* or "chastening" (cf. Hebrews 12:5,7f.).

15:1-8) and the absence of fruit (Mark 4:3-9,13-20) point to nondiscipleship. Indeed "many of his disciples went back, and walked no more with him" (John 6:66, KJV). "No man, having put his hand to the plow, and looking back, is fit for the kingdom of God" (Luke 9:62, KJV). Judas the betrayer, the "son of perdition," went the way of remorse and suicide (John 13:21-30; 17:12; Matthew 27:3-10), while Peter the denier repentantly returned to the allegiance of love (John 13:36- 38; 18:15-18,25-27; 21:15-17). Forgiveness of one's brother is to be until "seventy times seven" (Matthew 18:21f.). Matthew records a very specific saying concerning how to deal with an offending brother:

> If your brother sins against you, go and tell him his fault, between you and him alone. If he listens to you, you have gained your brother. But if he does not listen, take one or two others along with you, that every word may be confirmed by the evidence of two or three witnesses. If he refuses to listen to them, tell it to the church; and if he refuses to listen even to the church, let him be to you as a Gentile and a tax collector (Matthew 18:15-17).

Discipleship and non-discipleship stand as two clear alternatives like two distinct gates, two trees, or two builders (Matthew 7:13-27).

In the Acts of the Apostles the most specific example of discipline is not by action of the apostles or the Christian community but by divine or providential action in the sudden deaths of Ananias and Sapphira (Acts 5:1-11). Yet Peter did rebuke Simon the magician (Acts 8:18-24). However, decisions respecting church order predominate in the Acts. These include the selection of Matthias (Acts 1:21-26), the addition of new believers to the church in Jerusalem (Acts 2:41-47; 4:4; 5:14; 6:1,7), the commonality of possessions in the church at Jerusalem (Acts 2:44f.; 4:32-35), the choice of the seven (Acts 6:3-6), the reception of Saul of Tarsus by the "pillars" of the church in Jerusalem on recommendation of Barnabas (Acts 9:26-30; cf. Galatians 2:1-10), the setting apart of Barnabas and

Saul to the Gentile mission by the church at Antioch (Acts 13:1-3), the appointment[40] of elders by Barnabas and Paul in the new churches established on the first missionary journey (Acts 14:23), and the Jerusalem council (Acts 15:1-33).

The Pauline Epistles contain various instances of the negative aspects of church discipline together with numerous exhortations — ethical, unificatory, and doctrinal — basic to nurture and discipline. The specific references to disciplinary action include the withdrawal "from any brother who is living in idleness" and admonition of him as a "brother," not as an "enemy" (2 Thessalonians 3:6f.,14f.) and the restoration of a brother "overtaken in a fault" (Galatians 6:1f., KJV.). Of significance is Paul's apostolic insistence that an incestuous member of the church at Corinth be delivered "to Satan for the destruction of the flesh, that his spirit may be saved in the day of the Lord Jesus" (1 Corinthians 5:1-8). The principle is that the Christian fellowship is to "judge" those inside the church and to "drive out" the wicked person — "fornicator, or covetous, or an idolater, or a railer, or a drunkard, or an extortioner" from among them (1 Corinthians 5:9-13, KJV).

Paul's rebuke of the practice of Christians' taking their disputes to pagan courts was based on the idea that a wise member of the church should decide in such matters, for "the saints will judge the world" and even "angels" (1 Corinthians 6:1-8). Second Corinthians indicates that the Corinthian congregation by majority action had punished a brother who had led resistance to Paul's ministry. Paul calls for forgiveness, comfort, and love of the brother (2 Corinthians 2:5-11; 7:12). He claims to "have delivered to Satan" Hymenaeus and Alexander, who, "rejecting conscience ... have made shipwreck of their faith" (1 Timothy 1:19f.). Likewise, Paul counsels: "As for a man who is

---

[40] Calvin argued that *cheirotonesantes* indicated a vote, *Institutes of the Christian Religion*, IV, 3, 15, yet the word in this context may have lost its strict classical meaning and mean "appoint."

factious,[41] after admonishing him once or twice, have nothing more to do with him" (Titus 3:10).

Paul's ethical admonitions show the relationship of the Christian life to church discipline. Sanctification is defined in terms of abstaining from fornication (1 Thessalonians 4:1-8; 1 Corinthians 6:9-11,18- 20). Christians as sons of light are to walk in the light rather than in the darkness (1 Thessalonians 5:4-8; Romans 13:12 ff.; Ephesians 5:7-14). Christian liberty is not to be used "as an opportunity for the flesh"; the Christian is to be characterized by "the fruit of the Spirit" instead of "the works of the flesh" (Galatians 5:13-26). Those who persist in unrighteousness shall not be inheritors of God's kingdom (1 Corinthians 6:9f.; Ephesians 5:5). The problem concerning meat which had been sacrificed to idols led Paul to the principle, "'all things are lawful,' but not all things are helpful" (1 Corinthians 10:23). Responsible Christian liberty puts no stumbling block before weaker brethren (1 Corinthians 8:9-13; Romans 14:13-23). They who have been baptized into the death of Jesus Christ have been raised to "walk in newness of life," counting themselves "dead to sin and alive to God in Christ Jesus"; "free from sin," they have "become slaves of righteousness" (Romans 6:3f.,11,18). A Christian is one who has "put off the old man" and "put on the new man" (Colossians 3:9f.; Ephesians 4:22-24, KJV). Yet Paul regretfully reported that many live as "enemies of the cross of Christ," but the "manner of life" of Christians ought to be "worthy of the gospel of Christ" (Philippians 3:18f.; 1:27).

Paul admonished the Corinthians to overcome schisms or factionalism (1 Corinthians 1:10f.). Such a condition is indicative of "babes in Christ" (1 Corinthians 3:1). Both Jew and Gentile have been reconciled "to God in one body through the cross," for Christ creates "in himself one new man in place of the two" (Ephesians 2:16,15). Christians are to seek "to

---

[41] The Greek is *hairetikon*. "Heresy" was originally synonymous with schism and only later acquired the connotation of heterodoxy.

maintain the unity of the Spirit in the bond of peace" and to "attain to ... mature manhood" (Ephesians 4:3,13).

Doctrinal problems evoked warnings by Paul. Chief of these was the snare of incipient, and possibly Judaizing, gnosticism (Colossians 1:16; 2:8-10,16-23; 1 Timothy 4:1-4,7) which had both speculative and ethical aspects. False teachers of various kinds ought to be rejected (2 Timothy 3:4f.; Titus 1:10-14; 3:9; 2 Timothy 2:16-18; 4:3f.).

The non-Pauline epistles reveal similar emphases. God engages in a direct, divine discipline or chastening which indicates the sonship of those disciplined (Hebrews 12:5-11). Some "antichrists ... went out from us, but they were not of us; for if they had been of us, they would have continued with us; but they went out, that it might be plain that they all are not of us" (1 John 2:18f.). The turning back of a sinful brother from error to truth is greatly to be desired (James 5:19f.). Christians must beware of "an evil, unbelieving heart" and of being "hardened by the deceitfulness of sin" and must hold their "first confidence firm to the end" (Hebrews 3:12-14). They are to "be holy" even as God is "holy" and to "live as free men, yet without using ... freedom as a pretext for evil" (1 Peter 1:15f.; 2:16). Yet "there is sin which is mortal" (1 John 5:16). Unity and maturity are stressed. Christians are to "consider how to stir up one another to love and good works" and not to neglect "to meet together, as is the habit of some" (Hebrews 10:24f.). Some who are now "dull of hearing" and who take "milk, not solid food," ought to grow to maturity with its "solid food" (Hebrews 5:11-14). False teachers — docetist (1 John 4:1-3; 2 John 7-10), antinomian (Jude 4,8; 2 Peter 2:2,12-19), and speculative (2 Peter 2:1,10f.) — are to be avoided.

Similar warnings against false teachers were given to the churches of Asia — against Nicolaitans (Revelation 2:6,15), Balaamites (Revelation 2:14), the cult of Jezebel the prophetess (Revelation 2:20-23), and other false "apostles" (Revelation 2:2).

The motif of responsible discipline in the Christian community has been repeatedly emphasized during Christian history. The strict discipline[42] of the second and early third centuries, under pressure of growing laxity within and of imperial persecution from without, yielded to a public penitential discipline. Under such discipline there came to be no sin for which there could not be ultimate ecclesiastical remission.

Reaction to the prevailing leniency toward those who had denied the Christian faith during persecutions took the forms of Novatianism and Donatism. Admission to the Catholic Church at first involved a prebaptismal catechumenate, but this was eventually supplanted by infant baptism and subsequent confirmation. Pagan infiltration and state support accelerated the decline in the Church's standards.

Then came another reaction, monasticism. The monastic communities, whether under Pachomian, Basilian, or Benedictine rule, had a definite discipline, predicated on the dualism of those inside seeking perfection and those outside accommodating themselves to the world. The Irish monasteries led in inaugurating private penance. Hildebrandine reforms and the rise of orders of friars were efforts to renew discipline. Calvin's Geneva is a prime example of the pattern of discipline in the Protestant establishments of the major Reformers.[43] The free church tradition within Protestantism or what has been recently denominated as the "radical" wing of the Reformation, particularly in its formative period, magnified church discipline.

As early as 1524, Conrad Grebel and others of the Swiss Brethren admonished Thomas Müntzer, revolutionary Spiritualist in Saxony, "Go forward with the Word and establish

---

[42] Cf. Hermas' one post-baptismal repentance (*Shepherd,* II, 4, 3); Tertullian's "seven deadly sins," i.e., "idolatry, blasphemy, murder, adultery, fornication, false-witness, and fraud" (*Against Marcion,* IV, 9); and the three unforgivable or cardinal sins, i.e., idolatry or apostasy, murder, and adultery (cf. Tertullian, *Modesty,* 19).

[43] Cf. *Institutes of the Christian Religion,* IV, xi, 1-4; xii, 1-13; xx, 1-7.

a Christian church with the help of Christ and his rule, as we find it instituted in Matthew 18:15-18 and applied in the Epistles."[44] What seems to be the oldest Anabaptist confession, the Schleitheim Confession (Feb., 1527), probably fashioned under the leadership of Michael Sattler, deals with the nature of the church as a disciplined community of Christian brethren.[45] Article two refers to the use of the "ban" after two secret admonitions have failed.[46] Article three interprets participation in the Lord's Supper as being for "those who shall be united beforehand by baptism in one body of Christ" and who have no "fellowship with the dead works of darkness." Article four calls for evangelical separation "from the evil ... in the world." Article five defines the pastoral office, including disciplinary and edificatory functions. Article six teaches that the sword is not to be used to enforce church discipline. Recent scholarship has extracted from the Hutterite chronicle[47] another early Anabaptist document on church order, probably drawn up by Hans Schlaffer in 1527, "Church Discipline: How a Christian Ought to Live." These twelve brief articles include the practices of admonition, punishment of the disorderly, contribution for the poor, decent conduct, instruction of would-be members, and nonpublication of church decisions to nonmembers.[48]

Balthasar Hubmaier in 1527 argued that brotherly punishment is necessary for the well-being of the visible church, for even if

---

[44] "Letters to Thomas Müntzer by Conrad Grebel and Friends" (1524), *Spiritual and Anabaptist Writers*, ed. by George H. Williams and Angel M. Mergal (Philadelphia: The Westminster Press, 1957), p. 79.

[45] See English translation in W. L. Lumpkin, *Baptist Confessions of Faith* (Philadelphia: Judson Press, 1959), pp. 22-31.

[46] Cf. Matthew 18:15-17.

[47] I.e., *Geschicht-Buch der Hutterischen Brüder*, ed. by Rudolf Wolkan (Macleod, Alberta, and Vienna: Carl Fromme, 1923), pp. 60f. The document has also been found in an extant Hutterian codex in Canada. Cf. Robert Friedmann, "The Oldest Church Discipline of the Anabaptists," *The Mennonite Quarterly Review*, XXIX (April, 1955), (Goshen, Indiana: Mennonite Historical Society), 162-66.

[48] For English translation, cf. Lumpkin, *op. cit.*, pp. 31-35.

baptism and the Lord's Supper are rightly practiced, such ordinances are vain apart from brotherly punishment. Such punishment counteracts the antinomian opposition of "the old Adam." To refuse to engage in brotherly rebuke on the ground that one is a sinner is to destroy all brotherly admonition. Such rebuke follows from one's baptismal oath, by which one subjects himself to Christ and to the church.[49] Excommunication is to be only for "scandalous sin or public blasphemy" and is designed to prevent "eternal excommunication." It is based on the power of the keys which is given to the church by Christ and is to be surrendered to Christ at his *parousia*. Toward the excommunicated there should be an attitude of non-fellowship but without hate, use of force, or reckoning him an enemy. Such persons should, upon repentance, be received with joy and forgiveness even "seventy times seven."[50]

Ulrich Stadler of the Hutterites defended the right of "deacons of the Word" to administer discipline, including exclusion.[51] Pilgram Marpeck, elder among the South German Anabaptists, interpreted the "ban" in terms of "brotherly discipline" "conducive to betterment and repentance" and did not practice the more rigid "shunning" of the Mennonites.[52] Peter Ridemann, another Hutterite, taught immediate exclusion "without admonition" for the "gross and deadly sins" (cf. 1 Corinthians 5:11). Yet he recognized two kinds of exclusion,

---

[49] "Of Fraternal Punishment" (1527), *The Writings of Balthasar Hübmaier*, collected and photog. by W. O. Lewis and trans. by G. D. Davidson (Liberty, Mo.: Typescript, 1939), I, 328-45.

[50] "Of Christian Excommunication" (1527), *ibid.*, II, 581-602.

[51] "Cherished Instructions on Sin, Excommunication, and the Community of Goods" (c. 1537), *Spiritual and Anabaptist Writers*, pp. 276f. Such exclusion was economic and social as well as religious. Cf. *ibid.*, p. 274, fn. 4.

[52] John C. Wenger, "The Theology of Pilgram Marpeck," *Mennonite Quarterly Review*, XII (October 1938), pp. 251f., based on *Taufbüchlein* or *Vermahnung*, p. 263.

INTRODUCTION 13

one complete and the other more moderate, and taught readmission through the laying on of hands.[53]

Menno Simons wrote frequently on the ban, or excommunication, and shunning, or social avoidance of the excommunicated.[54] Although teaching that shunning should apply to husbands and wives and to parents and children, he did not follow the more rigorist Flemish Mennonites by insisting that such included "bed and board."[55] Menno early insisted upon threefold admonition without repentance prior to the ban, and the Waterlanders took this position.[56] But later he, like Ridemann, called for the use of the ban without admonition with regard to "openly offensive, carnal sinners." In this he was supported by Frisian and German Mennonites.[57]

"Evangelical separation" is one of the seven "ordinances" of the true church, according to Dietrich Philips.[58] The Waterland Confession of Rys and Gerritsz teaches that excommunication presupposes an antecedent divine judgment and that shunning should not necessitate withdrawal from marital privileges.[59] According to the unificatory Dordrecht Confession (1632),

---

[53] *Account of Our Religion, Doctrine and Faith*, trans. by Kathleen E. Hasenberg (Salop, England: Plough Publishing House, 1950), pp. 131-33.

[54] "A Kind Admonition on Church Discipline" (1541), "A Clear Account of Excommunication" together with "Some Questions and Answers on Church Discipline" (1550), "Reply to Gellius Faber" (1554), and "Instruction on Excommunication" (1558) in *The Complete Writings of Menno Simons*, trans. Leonard Verduin and ed. John C. Wenger (Scottdale, Pa.: Herald Press, 1956), pp. 407-18, 455-85, 723-34, 959-98.

[55] "A Clear Account of Excommunication," pp. 472, 478f.; cf. Williams in *Spiritual and Anabaptist Writers*, pp. 261f. Yet "Instruction on Excommunication," pp. 970-73, could be interpreted to include "bed and board."

[56] "The Waterland Confession" (1580), Art. 35, in Lumpkin, *op. cit.*, p. 62.

[57] "A Kind Admonition on Church Discipline" and "Instruction on Excommunication," pp. 411-13, 974-78. Cf. Lumpkin *op. cit.*, p. 42.

[58] "The Church of God" (c. 1560), in *Spiritual and Anabaptist Writers*, pp. 246-48.

[59] Arts. 35, 36, in Lumpkin, *op. cit.*, pp. 62-63.

shunning should never prevent a ministry to the needs or afflictions of those banned.[60]

The English Separatist and early English Baptist confessions of faith usually contained specific articles on church discipline as well as on the nature of the church and of the ministry. "A True Confession" (1596), the product of the Separatist refugee congregation in Amsterdam, specifies that each congregation shall admit and exclude members and shall, if necessary, depose and exclude ministers and that members, although being subject to censure, should not separate themselves for minor causes.[61] Mennonite influence on John Smyth and Thomas Helwys in respect to discipline seems very likely. Excommunication after the threefold admonition was adopted, and yet shunning was not to include "worldly business" or "civil societie."[62] Nor was it to prevent instruction, relief, or restoration of the excommunicated.[63] The last confession of the Smyth party, prior to union with the Waterlander Mennonites, mentions regeneration, the regenerates, or the new creation in twenty-one of its one hundred articles.[64]

The confessions of faith of English Baptist churches and associations, both General and Particular, reflect a concern for order and discipline. The practice of shunning was never fully accepted, and congregational polity became a concern, especially among Particular Baptists. The London Confession of 1644 identifies Christ's spiritual kingdom with the Church

---

[60] Art. 17, in Lumpkin, *op. cit.*, p. 77.

[61] Arts. 24, 23, 25, 36, in Lumpkin, *op. cit.*, pp. 89f., 94.

[62] "Short Confession of Faith in XX Articles of John Smyth" (1609), Arts. 17, 18; "A Short Confession of Faith" (1610), Arts. 33, 34; "A Declaration of Faith of English People Remaining at Amsterdam in Holland" (1611), Arts. 17, 18, in Lumpkin, *op. cit.*, pp. 101, 110f., 121.

[63] "Propositions and Conclusions Concerning True Christian Religion" (1612-14), Art. 80, in Lumpkin, *op. cit.*, p. 139.

[64] *Ibid.*, Arts. 41, 42, 44, 47, 49, 51-53, 56-63, 65, 73, 75, 81, 98, in Lumpkin, *op. cit.*, pp. 131-39, 142.

and affirms that this "Church, as it is visible to us, is a company of visible Saints, called & separated from the world, ... and joyned to the Lord, and each other, by mutuall agreement." Such saints are to live in Christ's "walled sheepfold and watered garden." To "every particular Congregation" and to the entirety of such a congregation is given the power of admission and exclusion. Every member is subject to censure by the congregation, but such power should be exercised "with great care and tendernesse."[65] General Baptists gave stress to the care of the poor and the material support of their ministers.[66] Excommunications should be reported to sister churches, and controversies not easily settled may be taken to them for assistance.[67] "The right and only way, of gathering Churches" is to be maintained, but profession of faith must be beautified "with a holy and wise conversation."[68] Particular Baptists warned churches and ministers not to receive members without "evident demonstration of the new birth, and the work of faith with power,"[69] yet acknowledged that "the purest Churches under heaven are subject to mixture, and error."[70] Particular Baptists taught that churches should submit problems of doctrine or administration to the association of churches for advice but denied that associations have "Church power" or "jurisdiction over the Churches."[71] General Baptists regarded their "general councils or assemblies" as having "lawful power

---

[65] Arts. 33, 34, 42, 43, in Lumpkin, *op. cit.,* pp. 165f., 168.

[66] "The Faith and Practise of Thirty Congregations" (1651), Arts. 57, 64, 65; "The True Gospel-Faith Declared According to the Scriptures" (1654), Arts. 19, 24; "The Standard Confession" (1660), Arts. 19, 16, in Lumpkin, *op. cit.,* pp. 184f., 194f., 230f.

[67] "The Faith and Practise of Thirty Congregations," Arts. 72, 70, in Lumpkin, *op. cit.,* pp. 186f.

[68] "The Standard Confession," Arts. 11, 14, in Lumpkin, *op. cit.,* pp. 228f.

[69] "The Somerset Confession" (1656), Art. 25, subd. 21, in Lumpkin, *op. cit.,* p. 211.

[70] "The Assembly or Second London Confession" (1677, 1688), Art. 26, subd. 3, in Lumpkin, *op. cit.,* p. 285.

[71] *Ibid.,* Art. 26, subd. 15, in Lumpkin, *op. cit.,* p. 289.

to hear, and determine" cases of appeal and "also to excommunicate." A threefold ministry was recognized, i.e., messengers, pastors, and deacons, and to such ministers was given the execution of threefold discipline, i.e., admonition, withdrawal, and excommunication.[72]

At the end of the seventeenth century Baptists began to do what had been done in the early years of the Anabaptist movement; namely, to formulate statements of church order or church discipline which were distinct from, though supplemental to, their general doctrinal confessions.

In 1697 Benjamin Keach, minister of the Horsleydown (Particular Baptist) Church, London, with the collaboration of his son Elias Keach, published a condensed version of the Second London Confession with additional articles on laying on of hands and on psalm and hymn singing, to which was attached "The Glory and Ornament of a True Gospel-constituted Church,"[73] a treatise on discipline largely anti-paedobaptist in emphasis.

After adopting in 1742 the Second London Confession with the addition of two articles, the Philadelphia Baptist Association authorized Jenkin Jones and Benjamin Griffith to compose "an abstract, or brief treatise concerning ... Discipline"[74] to be annexed to the confession. The work was done by Griffith, who reported that he used

> a small tract published by Mr. Elias Keach,[75] ... a manuscript left by ... Abel Morgan[76] ... deceased, ... in some cases

---

[72] "The Orthodox Creed" (1678), Arts. 39, 31, 34, in Lumpkin, *op. cit.*, pp. 327, 319f., 322f.

[73] Cf. Lumpkin, *op. cit.*, pp. 239-40. Brown University does not presently have a copy of this work by Elias Keach, although such is claimed by W. T. Whitley, ed., *A Baptist Bibliography* (London: The Kingsgate Press, 1916), I, 131.

[74] *A Confession of Faith* ... adopted by the Baptist Association, met at Philadelphia, September 25, 1742, ... [and] *A Short Treatise, etc.* (Philadelphia: S. C. Ustick, 1810), *Treatise*, p. 1. Hereafter cited as ST (Philadelphia).

[75] Possibly "The Glory and Ornament of a True Gospel-constituted Church."

consulted Dr. Owen[77] and Dr. Goodwin,[78] and in some things ... followed the agreement that our Association came to some years ago, especially concerning the admission and dismission of Members.[79]

The Philadelphia Association adopted this *Short Treatise* in 1743. A half century later a need for revision was in evidence. In 1795 the association appointed Samuel Jones to undertake the revision, and in 1797 a new treatise was approved.[80]

The Charleston Baptist Association, the oldest in the South,[81] adopted in 1767 the Philadelphia Confession of Faith with

---

[76] Probably Abel Morgan, Sr. (1673-1722), who seems only to have published a Bible concordance and a confession of faith, both in Welch. Cf. David Spencer, *The Early Baptists of Philadelphia* (Philadelphia: William Syckelmoore, 1877), pp. 48, 55.

[77] John Owen (1616-1683), Puritan theologian and Independent pastor, whose writings included "Eshcol, a Cluster of the Fruit of Canaan; Rules of Walking in Fellowship, with Reference to the Pastor or Minister That Watcheth for Our Souls," "A Brief Instruction in the Worship of God, and Discipline of the Churches of the New Testament," "An Inquiry into the Original Nature, Institution, Power, Order, and Communion of Evangelical Churches," and "The True Nature of a Gospel Church and Its Government," *The Works of John Owen*, ed. by Thomas Russell (London: Richard Baynes, 1826), XIX, 69-108, 463-568; XX, 65-250, 337-601.

[78] Thomas Goodwin (1600-1680), also a Puritan theologian and Independent pastor, the author of "The Government of the Churches of Christ" and "The Government and Discipline of the Churches of Christ," *The Works of Thomas Goodwin* (Edinburgh: James Nichol, 1865), XI, 1-484, 485-525.

[79] *ST*, p. 2.

[80] *A Confession of Faith ...* [and] *A Short Treatise of Church Discipline* adopted by the Sansom Street Baptist Church, Philadelphia (Philadelphia: Anderson and Meehan, 1818), p. 3. This 1818 printing resulted from the adoption in 1817 of Samuel Jones' discipline by Sansom Street Church with omission of the chapter on ruling elders. Citable as *TCD* (Philadelphia). For a comparison of ST and *TCD*, cf. Robert T. Handy, "The Philadelphia Tradition," in Winthrop Still Hudson, ed., *Baptist Concepts of the Church* (Philadelphia: Judson Press, 1959), pp. 30-52. For excerpts from ST and *TCD* on associations of churches, cf. Hudson, comp., "Documents on the Association of Churches," *Foundations*, IV (Oct., 1961), 332-39.

[81] Organization began on October 21, 1751, less than two years after the arrival in Charleston of Oliver Hart, formerly of Pennsylvania. Wood Furman, *A History of the Charleston Association of Baptist Churches in the State of South Carolina* (Charleston, S.C.: J. Hoff, 1811), pp. 7-9.

omission of the article on laying on of hands. The same year it appointed Oliver Hart[82] and Francis Pelot "to draw up a system of Discipline agreeable to Scripture, to be used by the Churches." These presented a draft of a discipline in 1772, and the association requested Morgan Edwards and David Williams to "assist the compilers in revising it." The resultant treatise was "examined" and "adopted" in 1773,[83] and together with the confession *A Summary of Church-Discipline*[84] was published in 1774. The *Summary* was published separately in 1783[85] in Wilmington, North Carolina, and in 1794[86] in Richmond, Virginia. Two thousand additional copies of this work were evidently printed in Charleston in 1794.[87] It was published

---

[82] Hart had been baptized by Jenkin Jones. Cf. Basil Manly, "A History of the First Baptist Church" in H. A. Tupper, ed., *Two Centuries of the First Baptist Church of South Carolina, 1683-1883* (Baltimore: R. H. Woodward & Co., 1889), pp. 102f.

[83] Furman, *op. cit.*, pp. 12f.

[84] *A Confession of Faith* ... [and] *A Summary of Church- Dicipline [sic]* Shewing the Qualifications and Duties of the Officers and Members of a Gospel-Church by the Baptist-Association in Charleston, S.C. (Charleston, S.C.: David Bruce, 1774). Hereafter cited as *SCD, 1774*.

[85] *A Summary of Church Discipline* ... (Wilmington, N.C.: James Adams, 1783). The editor has not been able to examine this printing, copies of which are in the Library of Congress and in the Samuel Colgate Collection, Colgate Rochester Divinity School, Rochester, New York.

[86] *A Summary of Church Discipline [sic]* ... (Richmond, Va.: John Dixon, 1794). This printing seems to be verbally identical with the original (1774) edition and does not contain the alterations found in the 1794 Charleston printing. Cf. fn. 60.

[87] *A Summary of Church-Discipline* ... 2nd edition (Charleston: Markland, McIver & Co., 1794). Hereafter cited as *SCD, 1794 (Charleston)*. Only a few minor verbal alterations distinguish this edition from *SCD, 1774*. Cf. Furman, *op. cit.*, p. 25.

INTRODUCTION 19

along with the Charleston Confession of Faith in 1813,[88] 1831,[89] and in 1850.[90] Subsequent Baptist confessions of faith in the United States have contained few explicit references to church discipline.[91] Several noteworthy books on church order and discipline by Baptists in the United States were written during the nineteenth century.[92]

The Charleston *Summary of Church Discipline* is the product of the Calvinistic Baptist tradition in which it was formulated.

---

[88] *A Confession of Faith* ... Second Charleston Edition ..., *A Summary of Church-Discipline* ... [and] *The Baptist Catechism* ... (Charleston, S.C.: Printed for the Charleston Baptist Association by J. Hoff, 1813). This edition adopted the slight verbal alterations of *SCD*, 1794 (Charleston), and corrected two of its four errors. This edition seems to have been the result of the decision of the Charleston Association in 1810 to "patronize the publication of the Confession of Faith, System of Discipline, and Catechism, in one volume; and to address the other Baptist associations in the State with a view of obtaining their concurrence," Furman, *op. cit.*, p. 34.

[89] *Baptist Confession of Faith and A Summary of Church Discipline*, to which is added an appendix. (Charleston: Printed by W. Riley for Daniel Sheppard, 1831). This edition of the *Summary* seems to be identical with that of 1813.

[90] *A Confession of Faith* ... Fourth Charleston Edition ... *A Summary of Church-Discipline* ..., [and] *The Baptist Catechism* ... (Raleigh, N.C.: Printed by B. Temple at the Primitive Baptist Office, 1850). This edition, evidently based on the 1813 and 1831 editions, has a few printing errors peculiar to itself.

[91] Cf. "Articles of Faith, Kehukee (Primitive) Baptist Association" (1777), Arts. 12, 13, 16, 17; "Principles of Faith of the Sandy Creek Association" (1816), Arts. 6, 7; "Terms of Union Between the Elkhorn and South Kentucky, or Separate, Associations" (1801), Arts. 10, 11; "New Hampshire Confession" (1833), Arts. 13, 14; "Articles of Faith of the Baptist Bible Union of America" (1923), Arts. 13, 14, in Lumpkin, *op. cit.*, pp. 356f., 358, 359, 365f., 388.

[92] E.g., William Crowell, *The Church Member's Hand-Book* (Boston: Gould and Lincoln, 1858); John Leadley Dagg, *A Treatise on Church Order* (Charleston, S.C.: Southern Baptist Publication Society, 1859); Edward Thurston Hiscox, *The Baptist Directory* (New York: Sheldon & Co., 1859; rev. ed., 1890); Patrick Hughes Mell, *Corrective Church Discipline* (Charleston, S.C.: Southern Baptist Publication Society, 1860); James Madison Pendleton, *Church Manual* (Philadelphia: American Baptist Publication Society, 1867); Williams Rutherford, *Church Members' Guide for Baptist Churches* (Atlanta: James P. Harrison & Co., 1885); William Wallace Everts, *Baptist Layman's Book* (Philadelphia: American Baptist Publication Society, 1887); and Hiscox, *The Standard Manual for Baptist Churches* (Philadelphia: American Baptist Publication Society, 1890).

This is revealed in the theological overtones of the document as well as by its quotations from John Gill, the well-known English Particular Baptist theologian.

While it belongs to the Calvinistic Baptist heritage, whose major fountain in America was Philadelphia, the *Summary* is to be differentiated from the *Short Treatise* at certain points. W. D. May[93] has found nine pertinent differences between the two documents.

"The *Summary* contains a more systematically thought out and applied theology than does the *Treatise*," says May. Use of the *Treatise* itself, dependence on Gill, a plurality of authors and revisers, and the greater length of time employed may help to explain this difference.

In constituting a church the *Treatise* emphasizes that candidates are "first orderly baptized," while the *Summary* calls for subscription to a written covenant and observance of the Lord's Supper.

The *Summary* alone specifically declares that women are not to share in the government of the congregation.

The *Summary* states that "ministers" are to lay on hands in the ordination of a minister, while the *Treatise* refers to "the hands of the presbytery of that church, or of neighbouring elders called and authorised by that church."[94]

The *Treatise* contains an article on ruling elders, while the *Summary* makes no mention of such.

The *Treatise* prescribes that elders should lay hands on candidates after the act of baptism, but on this the *Summary* does not speak.

---

[93] William David May, "The Philadelphia and Charleston Baptist Church Disciplines: A Theological Analysis" (Unpublished Th.M. Thesis, Southern Baptist Theological Seminary, Louisville, Ky., 1961), pp. 59-62.

[94] ST (Philadelphia), p. 6.

INTRODUCTION   21

While both teach ministerial support, the *Treatise* admits of the possibility that ministers may find it necessary to "betake to other secular employments to support themselves and families."[95]

The *Treatise* alone provides that, if and when a congregation "is informed that a member hath acted amiss, either in matters of faith or practice," and investigation of the same is in process by the elders, the member should be immediately suspended "from communion at the Lord's table."[96]

The *Summary*, following Gill, interprets the Pauline expression, deliverance "unto Satan for the destruction of the flesh" (1 Corinthians 5:5), as not applying to the modem practice of excommunication, while the *Treatise* interprets contemporary excommunications in terms of this expression.

The *Summary* is, to be precise, a document on church order and church discipline. Beginning with the distinction between the "universal Church" and "particular" churches (I, 1), the *Summary* defines the membership of particular churches (I, 2); the constitution of particular churches, including the procedure in constituting such (I, 3); and the government of particular churches (I, 4).

Then church officers, ministers and deacons, are discussed. Ministers are treated in respect to their appointment by Christ, qualifications, trial, ordination, authority, and duties (II, 1). The qualifications, choice, and duties of deacons follow (II, 2).

The reception of members is the third principal subject in the *Summary*. The qualifications of members include an experience of grace, a knowledge of divine things, becoming conduct, and baptism by immersion on profession of faith (III, 1). The discussion of admission of members embraces the majority vote of the congregation, instruction by the minister, the right hand

---

[95] *Ibid.*, p. 22.

[96] *Ibid.*, p. 26.

of fellowship, and union and communion. Also mentioned are "occasional communion" (a type of associate membership), removal of membership with the removal of residence, letters of commendation, and the reception of those suspended or excommunicated (III, 2).

The duties of church members are presented according to a fourfold division: toward ministers (IV, 1), toward deacons (IV, 2), toward fellow members (IV, 3), and toward the congregation (IV, 4).

The censures of the church are three: rebuke or admonition (V, 1), suspension (V, 2), and excommunication (V, 3). The nature of each censure and the types of offenses likely to warrant each censure are discussed. Excommunication is treated in greater detail: the importance of impenitence as a condition, excommunication as not self- inflictable, procedure, and ends or purposes.

Associations of churches are desirable and proper, are to be formed of "representatives" or "messengers" from the churches, and are advisory councils rather than superior judicatures. They are responsible for the admission of churches, are to follow proper procedures in transacting business, and should produce distinct benefits (VI).

A precise appraisal of the usage of the *Summary* by the churches comprising the Charleston Association is difficult to obtain. Evidences of the practice of church discipline by these and other South Carolina Baptist churches in the late eighteenth and early nineteenth centuries are numerous.[97] It is not clear whether the *Summary per se* influenced the practice of the churches and associations or whether the *Summary* merely reflects the practice which existed.

---

[97] Cf. Leah Townsend, *South Carolina Baptists, 1670-1805* (Florence, S.C.: Florence Printing Company, 1935), pp. 64, 90, 92, 93, 103, 112, 135, 164, 181, 186, 187, 192, 201, 206, 215, 224, 241, 249, 254, 291, 292, 293, 299.

The minutes of the Charleston Association from 1775 to 1825 indicate numerous instances of discipline in respect to ministers, baptism and the Lord's Supper, schism, ethical issues, and miscellaneous questions.[98] The circular letters of the Charleston Association from 1792 to 1810, though evidencing almost no direct dependence on the *Summary,* often dealt with subjects common to the *Summary.*[99]

During the pastorate of Richard Furman, Sr. (1787-1825) the First Church of Charleston practiced a quarterly public catechizing of the children of its members.[100] "The greatest care was exercised in guarding against premature professions of piety, and church discipline was ministered with conscientious faithfulness."[101]

The *Summary's* frequent citation of biblical passages makes relevant the question whether such passages were properly interpreted and applied to the subject matter of the *Summary.* Some of the citations are dubious in the light of contemporary biblical scholarship. The *Summary* is predicated on an allegorical interpretation of the Song of Solomon which affords proof-texts about Christ and his church.[102] Amos 3:3, which refers to Israel's walking with God, is cited in reference to Christian marriage within the church fellowship (IV, 3). Reference is made to Zechariah 11:10,14, which refers to the

---

[98] May, *op. cit.,* pp. 76-83.

[99] Furman, *op. cit.,* pp. 81-238.

[100] Oliver F. Gregory, "History of the Sunday-Schools of the Church," in H. A. Tupper, ed., *Two Centuries of the First Baptist Church of South Carolina, 1683-1883* (Baltimore: R. H. Woodward & Co., 1889), pp. 237f. The Sunday school was begun in 1816 (p. 236).

[101] Anonymous, "Biography of Richard Furman, Sr.," in *ibid.,* p. 146. This biography of 1883 was probably composed by J. C. Furman on the basis of written sources. Cf. Harvey T. Cook, *A Biography of Richard Furman* (Greenville, S.C.: Baptist Courier Job Rooms, 1913), preface.

[102] Song of Solomon 6:9 (I,1); 8:8 (II,1); 4:12 (IV,4); 8:8 (VI).

breaking of the two staffs, "Beauty" and "Bands" (KJV),[103] probably the annulling of the covenant with Israel and the deliverance to internal strife, in order to support the distinction between suspension and excommunication (V, 2). Psalm 22:22 appears rather than a New Testament text related to the forgiveness of Peter (V, 3). Psalm 122:6-9 and Psalm 84:4,10, which refer to Jerusalem and its temple, are cited in reference to prayer for and attendance upon the meetings of Christian congregations (IV, 4).

In the same vein, a minister's obligation to join a particular church before being called as pastor is based on Acts 1:21, which refers to the companions of the apostles and eyewitnesses of Jesus' resurrection (II, 1). The assembling of "the multitude of disciples" by the twelve apostles for the selection of the "seven" (Acts 6:2) is cited in support of obligatory attendance of church meetings (V, 1). A Pauline reference to the Roman legal practice of confronting the accused with his accusers and affording him opportunity for self-defense (Acts 25:16) is used in support of the Christian's obligation not to take up an evil report against another (IV, 3). Many exegetes interpret 1 Corinthians 5:5 to refer to church discipline, but the *Summary*, following John Gill, affirms that this was an apostolic act, not performed by churches (V, 3). First Corinthians 5:12, which distinguishes Christians from non-Christians, is hardly a valid prooftext for congregational polity (I, 4). The *Summary* cites Ephesians 6:18-20, in which Paul asks fellow Christians to pray for him that he might speak boldly, in connection with the duty of church members to submit themselves to their ministers (IV, 1). Divine instruction of Moses in respect to the building of the tabernacle (Hebrews 8:5) is cited in support of the minister's obligation to administer the gospel ordinances biblically (II, 1). Revelation 3:17, a reference to material wealth leading to self-sufficiency, is related to a church's independence from a Baptist association which indicates self-sufficiency (VI).

---

[103] "Grace" and "Union" in RSV.

The beginning of what appears to be a renewal of a committed, disciplined churchmanship is one of the facts of contemporary Christianity. Those who stand in the heritage of "free church" Protestantism are being challenged to recover their classic covenant or consensus and its corollary, a committed, disciplined church.[104] Freedom, it must be realized, was only half the free church platform, for order or discipline was the other half. Some who stand in the heritage of "state church" or right-wing Protestantism likewise are calling for a renewal of discipline.[105] Reflection upon church history makes evident the fact that small committed, disciplined groups of Christians have often been instruments of religious and moral renewal, whether Roman Catholic monastic communities and religious orders or Protestant separatist fellowships.[106]

What can and should be the manner of such renewal of disciplined discipleship? Some have found the answer in newly structured Christian cell groups. Some of these, such as Scotland's Iona Community, combine summertime participation in a separated community with wintertime involvement in the social order.[107] Others have constituted new congregations on a strict standard of membership. An example of this is the Church of the Saviour, Washington, D.C.

---

[104] Elton Trueblood, *Alternative to Futility* (New York: Harper & Brothers, 1948), pp. 82-103; Franklin Hamlin Littell, *The Free Church* (Boston: Starr King Press, 1957), esp. pp. 113-31; Trueblood, *The Yoke of Christ and Other Sermons* (New York: Harper & Brothers, 1958).

[105] Geddes MacGregor, *The Coming Reformation* (Philadelphia: The Westminster Press, 1960), esp. pp. 63-84; cf. Dietrich Bonhoeffer, *The Cost of Discipleship*, trans. R. H. Fuller (2d ed.; New York: The Macmillan Co., 1959).

[106] Trueblood, *Alternative to Futility*, pp. 44-57; Chad Walsh, *Early Christians of the 21st Century* (New York: Harper & Brothers, 1950), p. 173.

[107] Cf. Alexander Miller, "The Iona Community: An Experiment in Catholicity and Contemporaneity," *Theology Today*, VI (July, 1949), 224-34. On the Taizé Community in France, cf. Malcolm Boyd, "The Taizé Community," *Theology Today*, XV (Jan., 1959), 488-506.

Most Christians concerned about such renewal will find their best channel to be the congregation of which they are now members.[108] Some congregations are writing new church covenants and giving to the covenant major emphasis.[109] Trueblood calls for "orders" or groups of the "New Seventy" who will participate in the "abolition of the laity" and reformation of the church from within.[110] Robert A. Raines has described the combination of a sixfold congregational discipline (corporate worship, daily prayer, Bible reading and study, giving of money, service, and witness) with *koinonia* groups within the Aldersgate Methodist Church, Cleveland, Ohio.[111]

Professing Christians who are wary of a renewal of discipline should recall the role of discipline in the history of Communism. At the Second Congress of the Social Democratic Party in Russia in 1903, a split occurred between the Bolsheviks led by Lenin and the Mensheviks.

> The main difference concerned the organization of the party. In Lenin's view the party must be the "vanguard of the proletariat." It must lead the working class, as the working class must lead other classes into revolution.... The party must be a band of "professional revolutionaries," bound by an iron discipline. Quality must come before quantity. No one must be admitted to the party who would not completely subject himself to its leaders and put the claims of the party on his time and efforts before all others.[112]

---

[108] Trueblood, *The Yoke of Christ*, pp. 125f.

[109] For example, the Watts Street Baptist Church, Durham, N.C., and the University Baptist and Olin T. Binkley Memorial Baptist churches, Chapel Hill, N.C. Cf. William L. Hendricks, "The Church Covenant: Is It Accurate? Is It Adequate?" *The Baptist Program* (Feb., 1961), 24, 27, 29.

[110] *The Yoke of Christ*, pp. 118-27, 138-49.

[111] Robert A. Raines, *New Life in the Church* (New York: Harper & Brothers, 1961), esp. pp. 59-64, 78-87.

[112] Hugh Seton-Watson, *From Lenin to Malenkov* (New York: Frederick A. Praeger, 1953), p. 24.

INTRODUCTION

A frank appraisal of the contemporary Christian situation leads to the recognition of numerous problems connected with the renewal of church discipline. Some object on the ground that our Lord said "Judge not, that you be not judged" (Matthew 7:1). Others, while acknowledging that discipline is inherent in the New Testament, doubt the propriety of its present-day recovery. Still others point to the abuses of church discipline in its era of decline and abandonment.

Those who would lead in the renewal of discipline must be thoroughly convinced of its terrible urgency. Both positive nurture and negative censures, both "front door" and "back door" discipline are needed. The reluctance of the majority in many congregations will continue to be a reality, and discipline initiated and administered solely by the minister would be a travesty of congregationalism. The indifference of other churches and the continuation of "free and easy" church membership should not be deterrents.

Probably the greatest problem in the recovery is the avoidance of a neo-Pharisaic legalism. There must be no code of sins externally conceived, and sin must be viewed in its depth and its manifold expressions. Stated affirmatively, church discipline must be redemptive in purpose and not merely punitive. Grace and forgiveness must always be operative. The restoration of the offending brother must be of equal importance with the purity of the church. Anything less cannot be squared with our Lord and the New Testament.

The republication of the Charleston Baptist *Summary of Church Discipline* has as its major purpose the encouragement of the renewal of a proper church discipline through study of an important document in the history of Baptist church discipline. This, however, is by no means to imply that the *Summary*, as it is, should be adopted by twentieth-century Baptist churches. Its restriction of participation in congregational business to male members and insistence upon the silence of women in church meetings is one obvious aspect of the *Summary* to which contemporary objections would be raised.

The *Summary*, an eighteenth-century document of theological and historical but not literary importance, is at times not easily perceptible to the twentieth-century reader. Hence the editor has sought to make the document more readable either by slight alterations of the text such as dividing long sentences and altering archaic uses of pronouns and other words or by explanatory footnotes. Faithfulness to the meaning of the original has been the objective in making editorial alterations. Although the Revised Standard Version has been used in this introduction except where otherwise indicated, in the text itself the biblical quotations from the King James Version are retained.

A SUMMARY OF CHURCH-DICIPLINE.

SHEWING THE

QUALIFICATIONS and DUTIES, of the Officers and Members, of a Gospel-Church.

BY

The BAPTIST-ASSOCIATION,

IN

CHARLESTOWN, SOUTH-CAROLINA.

For this Cause left I thee in Crete, that thou shouldst set in order the Things that are wanting. Tit. i. 5.
See that thou make all Things according to the Pattern shewed to thee in the Mount, Heb. viii. 5.

CHARLESTOWN,
PRINTED BY DAVID BRUCE.
MDCCLXXIV.

(Facsimile of original title page)

A

SUMMARY

OF

CHURCH-DICIPLINE.

SHEWING THE QUALIFICATIONS and *DUTIES*, of the Officers and Members, of a Gospel-Church.

BY

THE BAPTIST-ASSOCIATION,
IN CHARLESTOWN, SOUTH-CAROLINA.

For this Cause left I thee in Crete, that thou shouldest set in Order the Things that are wanting. Titus 1:5.

See that thou make all Things according to the Pattern shewed to thee in the Mount, Hebrews 8:5.

CHARLESTOWN,
PRINTED BY DAVID BRUCE. MDCCLXXIV.

Text of the Charleston Discipline

PREFACE

The following *Summary of Church Discipline*, being designed chiefly for the benefit of the poor and unlearned, is contracted into a very narrow compass and exhibited in the plainest language. This, with whatever defects it has, will require the candor of the more learned and intelligent.

To remove in some measure the ignorance of but too many church members about discipline was the principal motive for engaging in this work.

We mean not to impose our sentiments on any person whatever, or to anathematize those who differ from us in opinion. The Word of God, and no human composition, is the standard by which our principles and conduct must be tried.

Nevertheless, we hope this small piece may be of some use for the right understanding of God's Word, with regard to the points treated on; and we desire that the Scriptures referred to may be carefully consulted, to see whether these things be true.

Some may say, "There is no call[113] for this publication, seeing there is such a valuable treatise on church discipline,[114] published some years ago by the Philadelphia Association."

We mean not to depreciate the value of that piece; it has merited much from the Baptist churches; but it is out of print, and we apprehend not so explicit as this; besides, some things therein appear to us exceptionable. However, we have borrowed many hints from it and we are greatly indebted to the late learned,

---

[113] I.e., need or reason.

[114] The reference is actually to *A Short Treatise, etc.* (1743).

pious, and judicious Dr. Gill for what is taken from his *Exposition* and *Body of Divinity*.[115]

May the great Head of the church bless this feeble attempt to promote his honor and the welfare of his churches.

A SUMMARY OF CHURCH DISCIPLINE

CHAPTER I. — *Of a True and Orderly Gospel Church*

1. God in every age hath had, has, and will have a church or people in the world, consisting of a greater or less number and subsisting under various forms and in diverse circumstances (Acts 7:38; Ephesians 3:21).

The catholic or universal church, considered collectively, forms one complete and glorious body (Song of Solomon 6:9), called Christ's mystical body, of which he is the Head (Colossians 1:18; Ephesians 1:22). This is the general assembly and church of the firstborn, which are written in heaven (Hebrews 12:23).

Under the Old Testament dispensation the church was pretty much confined to family or nation; but under the present administration Christ gathers to himself a people from among all nations (Matthew 28:19,20). And being thus gathered by the power of Christ in the gospel, it becomes their duty to unite in distinct churches (Acts 2:41,47) that they may walk together in all the commandments and ordinances of the Lord blameless. Hence we find that under the gospel, churches were settled wherever there was a sufficient number of converts for that purpose (Revelation 2-3).

A particular gospel church consists of a company of saints, incorporated by a special covenant into one distinct body and meeting together in one place for the enjoyment of fellowship

---

[115] John Gill, *An Exposition of the New Testament* (2 vols.; London, 1852), *A Complete Body of Doctrinal and Practical Divinity* (3 vols.; London, 1796).

with each other and with Christ their Head in all his institutions to their mutual edification and the glory of God through the Spirit (2 Corinthians 8:5; Acts 2:1).

2. The temple of the Lord is not to be built with dead but living materials (1 Peter 2:5). None has a right to church membership but such as Christ will own as his sincere followers at the last decisive day, whatever pretensions they may make to an interest in his favor (Matthew 7:22,23). Except a man be born again, he has no right to enter into the kingdom of God nor into a gospel church (John 3:3). Christ is a living Head and will have none but living members in his mystical body (John 15:6).

3. The constitution of churches is plainly supposed (Acts 2:47; Matthew 18:17, etc.), and it is necessary, in order that the disciples of Christ may enjoy the ordinance of the Lord's Supper, which is a church ordinance, that they watch over one another, warn the unruly, and lay censures on disorderly and impenitent persons.

The Scriptures do not absolutely determine the number of persons necessary to constitute a church; but, as our Lord has said, "For where two or three are gathered together in my name, there am I in the midst of them" (Matthew 18:20), it should seem as if that number of godly persons might, at least in some urgent cases, form a church essential, though not a church complete or duly organized, for lack of officers. Experience has sometimes proved that such small beginnings have been succeeded with a large increase, consistent with that encouraging promise, "A little one shall become a thousand, and a small one a strong nation" (Isaiah 60:22).

A gospel church is not national, but congregational. This was evidently the case in the apostolic age; hence Paul sent a general epistle to the several churches in Galatia (Galatians 1:1-2), and our Lord himself ordered epistles to be written to the seven distinct churches in Asia (Revelation 2-3).

With regard to the manner of constituting a church, it must be by the consent and desire of the parties concerned; and it will be expedient to call in a minister or ministers, if to be had, to assist on that important occasion. The parties being met fasting,[116] the solemnity ought to be opened by fervent prayer to God (Philippians 4:6); next, a sermon suitable to the occasion should be preached; and then, for the mutual satisfaction of every individual, a strict inquiry should be made into their experience of a work of grace in their hearts, their soundness in the doctrines of faith, and the goodness of their lives and conversations;[117] unless, as members of churches, they come honorably recommended for that purpose. Being thus satisfied with each other's graces[118] and qualifications and united in the bond of love, they should give up themselves to the Lord and to one another by the will of God (2 Corinthians 8:5) by subscribing a written covenant consistent with the Word of God (Isaiah 44:5), thereby binding and obliging themselves to be the Lord's, to walk in all his commands and ordinances, and in all respects to behave toward each other as brethren, agreeable to the spiritual relation into which they now enter.

Being thus united in one body under Christ their Head, they become and are to be deemed a church essential, founded on the gospel plan. Let them then ratify their engagements by a participation of the Lord's Supper and so conclude the solemnity.

4. A church thus constituted has the keys, or power of government, within itself, having Christ for its Head and his law for its rule. It has the power and privilege of choosing its own officers (Acts 6:3; 13:2), exercising its own discipline (Matthew 18:17), and of administering the Word and ordinances, for the

---

[116] I.e., the persons assembling having fasted.

[117] As in sixteenth-century KJV usage, so here "conversation" may mean manner of life, not merely speech. Yet the meaning as speech appears in IV, 3.

[118] The words "graces" and "gracious" are used in the *Summary* to refer to the reception of God's saving grace, not to affability or comeliness.

edification and comfort of its members (Acts 2:46). All of these, with every other act of discipline, each distinct church may exercise without being subject to the cognizance of any other church, presbytery, synod, or council whatever (1 Corinthians 5:12; Matthew 18:17).

Churches being vested with such power ought to use it with prudence lest they dishonor Christ and his cause or wound their fellow members (1 Corinthians 10:31; Romans 15:2). To guard against this, church business should be debated deliberately with humility and moderation so that, if possible, the members may be unanimous in all their determinations. Nevertheless, when this unanimity cannot be attained, a majority of the male members may determine and the minority ought peaceably to submit. This appears not only from that general rule "submitting yourselves one to another in the fear of God" (Ephesians 5:21), but more clearly from "Sufficient to such a man is this punishment, which was inflicted of many" (2 Corinthians 2:6), which "many" supposes a majority. In the original it is *hupo ton pleionon*, "by the more," the greater or major part. This plainly points out a decision by a majority.

Female members may, when called upon, act as witnesses in a church and, when aggrieved, are to make known their case, either in person or by a brother, and must have a proper regard paid them. But they are excluded from all share of rule or government in the church (1 Corinthians 14:34-35; 1 Timothy 2:11-12).

CHAPTER II. — *Of Church Officers*

The ordinary officers of the church, and the only ones now existing, are ministers and deacons (Philippians 1:1). In the first gospel churches there were other officers such as apostles, prophets, and evangelists (1 Corinthians 12:28; Ephesians 4:11) who were endowed with extraordinary gifts, which were then necessary for the confirmation of the gospel but have since become extinct.

1. Ministers of the gospel, who are frequently called elders, bishops, pastors, and teachers, are appointed by Christ to the highest office in the church and therefore need peculiar qualifications such as are pointed out (1 Timothy 3:2-7 and Titus 1:5-10).

As they have the charge of souls and are leaders in the house of God, churches cannot be too careful in choosing men to the ministerial function. They ought to be men fearing God, being born again of the Spirit, found in the faith, and of blameless lives and conversations, as is becoming to the gospel of Christ, having fervent desires to glorify God and save souls (John 3:10; 2 Timothy 1:13; 1 Timothy 3:2; Romans 9:3; 10:1).

A church having no minister should look among its own members to see if there be any who seem to have promising gifts and graces for that great work. If such a one is found, he is to be put on private trial for a season; on finding that he is promising and that they[119] are edified by his preaching, they may call him to preach in public. After this, if it should appear that his rod, like Aaron's, buds, blossoms, and bears fruit, he is to be set apart by ordination that he may perform every part of the sacred function (Acts 13:2-3). But should no such person be found in the church, it is the duty of a sister church, if possible, to supply them (Song of Solomon 8:8). And if a person who is a member of another church be approved and inclined to accept a call from them, he must first become a member with them, so that they may choose him from among themselves (Acts 1:21). Thus were deacons chosen (Acts 6:3).

The candidate having accepted the call of the church, they proceed to his ordination, which is to be done in the following manner. If there is not a sufficient presbytery in the church, neighboring elders are to be called and authorized to perform that service. The day is set apart by fasting and prayer (Acts

---

[119] "They" is used here and in succeeding sentences to refer to the members of the church considered collectively.

13:2-3; 14:23). The elders, i.e., ministers, must be satisfied with regard to the gifts, graces, soundness of principles, and becoming life and conversation of the candidate. The church is to meet and give their suffrage[120] for his ordination. A sermon is to be preached on the occasion. The candidate is to declare his willingness and inward call to take on himself the sacred office (1 Corinthians 9:16). A public confession of his faith will be required. Then the ministers lay their hands on his head and by prayer set him apart to the great work of the ministry. This done, they give him the right hand of fellowship (Galatians 2:9), and then one of the ministers publicly gives him a charge or directory[121] how to behave himself in the house of God (2 Timothy 4:5). The solemnity is concluded by prayer, singing, and a blessing on the whole congregation.

A minister, being ordained, has authority from Christ to preach the gospel and baptize believers in any part of the world where God in his providence may call him. But if he should be called unto and accept the pastoral charge of any particular church, he will be more immediately confined to them and they to him (1 Peter 5:1-3).

Persons thus commissioned are to attend to their work with all possible engagedness, as it becomes those who have the charge of souls. They must give themselves up to study, prayer, and meditation (1 Timothy 4:14-16), that they may be workmen who need not be ashamed (2 Timothy 2:15). They must be instant in season and out of season, preaching the pure doctrines of the gospel (2 Timothy 1:13; 4:2). They are to feed the Lord's flock with spiritual bread (Acts 20:28) and to preach with the view of bringing souls to Christ, not for the sake of honor or filthy lucre. They are not to lord it over God's heritage, but to be patient and tenderhearted (2 Timothy 2:25). They are to

---

[120] I.e., to vote.

[121] I.e., directive.

watch over the flock, to "comfort the feebleminded"[122] (1 Thessalonians 5:14); to sound the alarm to the wicked and obstinate (Ezekiel 3:17-18); and to set their faces like flints against prophaneness and every vice.

They should often visit the flock committed to their charge, to know the state of their souls, that they may speak a word in season to them, catechize the youths, instruct the ignorant, and pray with and for them. They are especially to visit the sick and those who are otherwise afflicted (Ezekiel 34:4).

They are to administer the ordinances of the gospel in a strict conformity to the Word of God (Hebrews 8:5), to preside in the affairs of the church, and to see that strict discipline is duly executed therein (Hebrews 13:7,17). In a word, they are to be examples to the flock — "in word, in conversation, in charity, in spirit, in faith, in purity" (1 Timothy 4:12).

2. As it is the duty of ministers more particularly to give themselves to prayer and to the ministry of the Word, God has appointed officers to be employed in the inferior services of the church, namely deacons, whose qualifications are pointed out (Acts 6:3; 1 Timothy 3:8-13).

Deacons are likewise to be chosen by the suffrage of the church from among its own members, and, being first proved, are to be set apart to that office by prayer and laying on of hands (Acts 6:2-6).

The office of a deacon is to relieve the minister from the secular concerns of the church; hence they are called "helps" (1 Corinthians 12:28). Their business is to serve tables; as

> the table of the Lord, by providing the bread and wine for it; receiving both from the minister, when blessed, and distributing them to the members; and collecting from them for the poor, and they[123] defraying the charge; and observing

---

[122] This is KJV; ASV and RSV more accurately translate the word "fainthearted."

[123] Gill has "the" instead of "they." Cf. fn. 124.

what members whom they are to admonish who are missing at the ordinance; and if their admonitions are not regarded to report it to the church. They are likewise to serve the minister's table, by taking care that he has a sufficient competency for his support; and it belongs to them to stir up the members of the church to their duty in communicating to him; and what they receive of them, they are to apply to his use; and also they are to serve the poor's table, to whom they are to distribute of the church's stock with all impartiality, simplicity, cheerfulness, and sympathy.[124]

By the faithful discharge of their office they shall "purchase to themselves a good degree, and great boldness in the faith" (1 Timothy 3:13).

CHAPTER III — *Of Receiving Persons to Church Membership*

A church thus founded on the Scripture plan ought to observe good order, as in all other cases, so also in the admission of members into their community.

1. Every well-regulated society requires qualifications in its members; much more should a church of Jesus Christ be careful that none be admitted into its communion but such as are possessed of those prerequisites pointed out in the Scriptures.

They must be truly gracious persons. None is fit material of a gospel church without having first experienced an entire change of nature. "Verily I say unto you, except ye be converted, and become as little children, ye shall not enter into the kingdom of heaven" (Matthew 18:3). By this is intended a gospel church state,[125] as the context clearly shows. To the same purpose is John 3:5. Christ's church is a spiritual house, built up of "lively

---

[124] Gill, *Exposition*, I, 840.

[125] The term "gospel church state" or "church state" was an eighteenth-century free church expression, meaning the condition of being constituted a Christian congregation. William Carey stated that Paul the apostle on the returning phase of his first missionary journey "formed" the converts "into a church state," *An Enquiry into the Obligations of Christians to Use Means for the Conversion of the Heathens* (Leicester, 1792; facsimile edition, London: Baptist Missionary Society, 1942), p. 21.

stones," i.e., of living souls (1 Peter 2:5). By nature we are "dead in trespasses and sins," and Christ doth not place such dead materials in his spiritual building. It is certain that the Ephesian church was not composed of such materials (Ephesians 2:1). The members of the church at Rome were "the called of Jesus Christ" (Romans 1:6), "called... out of darkness into" the Lord's "marvellous light" (1 Peter 2:9), "called to be saints" (Romans 1:7), as were the members of the church at Corinth (1 Corinthians 1:2), and the churches in general are called "churches of the saints" (1 Corinthians 14:33). The members of the church at Colossae are denominated not only "saints" but "faithful brethren in Christ" (Colossians 1:2), or true believers in him. None but such has a right to ordinances (Acts 8:37). Without faith none discerns the Lord's body in the Supper and consequently must eat and drink unworthily (1 Corinthians 11:29). Indeed, "without faith it is impossible to please" God (Hebrews 11:6).

The Church of England, in her Articles, defines a gospel church as "a congregation of faithful men, in which the pure Word of God is preached, and the Sacraments be duly ministered."[126] Of such "faithful men" or believers in Christ was the first church at Jerusalem composed (Acts 2:41; 5:14). Those whom "the Lord added to the church" were "such as should be saved" (Acts 2:47). Let those look to it who make the church of Christ a harlot by opening the door of admission so wide as to permit unbelievers, unconverted, and graceless persons to crowd into it without control.

They should be persons of some competent knowledge of divine and spiritual things, who have not only knowledge of themselves, of their lost state by nature, and of the way of salvation by Christ, but have some degree of knowledge of God in his nature, perfection, and works; of Christ in his person as the Son of God, of his proper deity, of his incarnation, and of his offices as prophet, priest, and king; of justification by his

---

[126] "The Thirty-nine Articles of the Church of England," Art. 19.

righteousness, pardon by his blood, satisfaction by his sacrifice, and his prevalent intercession of the Spirit of God — his person, offices, and operations; and of the important truths of the gospel and doctrines of grace. Or how otherwise should the church be the pillar and ground of truth?[127]

Their lives and conversations ought to be such as "becometh the gospel of Christ" (Philippians 1:27); that is, holy, just, and upright (Psalm 15:1-2); if their practice contradicts their profession they are not to be admitted to church membership. Holiness is becoming to the Lord's house forever (Psalm 93:5).

These ought to be truly baptized in water, i.e., by immersion, upon a profession of their faith, agreeable to the ancient practice of John the Baptist and the apostles of our Lord Jesus Christ (Matthew 3:6; John 3:23; Romans 6:4; Acts 8:36-38). It is allowed by all that baptism is essential to church communion and ought to precede it; there is not one instance in the Word of God of any being admitted without it; the three thousand penitents, after they had "gladly received" the Word, "were baptized";[128] and then, and not before, were added to the church. Also, the first church at Samaria consisted of men and women baptized by Philip, they believing what he said concerning the kingdom of God. And Lydia and her household and the jailor and his, being baptized upon their faith, laid the foundation of the church at Philippi. The church at Corinth was begun with persons who, hearing the Word, believed and were baptized. The church at Ephesus was first formed by some disciples baptized in the name of the Lord Jesus (Acts 8:12; 16:15,33; 18:8; 19:5). So the members of the churches at Rome, Galatia, and Colossae were baptized persons (Romans 6:3-4; Galatians 3:27; Colossians 2:12).

2. Persons making application are to be admitted into the communion of a church by the common suffrage of its

---

[127] Cf. 1 Timothy 3:15.

[128] Cf. Acts 2:41.

members, who must first be satisfied that these have the qualifications laid down in the preceding section. For this purpose candidates must come under examination before the church. If it should happen that they do not give satisfaction, they should be set aside until a more satisfactory profession is made (1 Timothy 6:12).

It may be that one or two of the members of the church have conceived a prejudice against a person applying for fellowship. In this case they are to be duly heard and if their objections are of sufficient weight the candidate must be set aside; if not, the majority of voices ought in all reason to decide it.

When the church concludes that the person applying for membership may be admitted, the minister is to acquaint him with the rules and orders of God's house. Upon his promising, covenanting, and agreeing strictly to observe them, as assisted by the Spirit of God, the minister, in behalf of the church, is to give him the right hand of fellowship and to receive him as a member into union and full communion with that particular church. Thereby he becomes entitled to all the rights and privileges thereof (Colossians 2:19; Romans 15:7; 2 Corinthians 8:5).

If a member should desire transient or occasional communion in any church to which he does not belong and if it be well known that he is an orderly person, he may be admitted to the Lord's table; but he should have nothing to do with the government of the church, unless his advice and assistance be asked. But a person unknown should by no means be admitted without a satisfactory letter of recommendation from the church to which he belongs.

When a member removes his residence nearer to another church of the same faith and order, he is bound in duty to procure a letter of dismission from the church to which he belongs (Acts 18:27). And the church to which he is removed is bound in duty to receive him into union and full communion, unless it should appear that he is either immoral in his life or unsound in his

BAPTIST CHURCH DISCIPLINE 45

principles. But let it be remembered that he continues to be a member of his own church from whence he came until he is received into the church to which he is removing (Acts 9:26-28). That it is the duty of a believer to give himself as a member of an orderly church nearest his place of residence, or which he can most conveniently attend, appears plain from the following considerations: (1) by the neglect of this duty he will deprive himself of the edification, comfort, loving instruction, watchful care, and faithful admonitions of his fellow members; (2) it would give room to suspect that he was impatient of that restraint which every humble member deems his mercy;[129] (3) it would seem as if he aimed at screening himself from necessary contributions, or from church discipline; (4) such a neglect casts a manifest contempt on the church and ministry near which he resides; (5) were this conduct to be allowed and to become general, it would cause great confusion among the churches; and as such a practice can suit none but careless and disorderly persons, the church to which they belong ought to admonish them, and if they still persist, to censure them.

The same reasons hold good against those who require a dismission from the church to which they belong unto one more remote. If one member may be so dismissed, another may — even officers of the church as well as others. To dismiss a member to the world at large would be yet more preposterous and ought never to be done in any other way but by excommunication. The usual plea for such an unreasonable request is either that they cannot profit under such a ministry or that the concerns of the church are not properly managed. The truth is that pride is generally at the bottom of such desires, for an humble Christian will esteem others better than himself, bear

---

[129] The use of "mercy" is obscure. It probably is related to an obsolete use as a synonym for "amercement," a payment or penalty imposed by a sovereign or a court (cf. *The Oxford English Dictionary, in loco*). The meaning would then be that a true ("humble") church member recognizes submission to the discipline of the church as a requirement ("mercy") imposed by constituted authority, i.e., by Christ himself.

with the infirmities of the weak, and pray and hope to find a blessing where Providence casts his lot.

It sometimes happens that an orderly member is called by Providence to remove, but, like Abraham (Hebrews 11:8), knows not whither. In such case the church to which he belongs ought to furnish him with a letter of commendation, permitting him to join any church of the same faith and order, where Providence may cast his lot (Colossians 4:10). On his being admitted into any such church, he is dismissed from the church of which he was a member and notice thereof should be given to the latter as soon as possible.

Members who have been suspended or excommunicated by the church and who give satisfactory evidence of their repentance are to be cautioned against the evils of which they were guilty. Upon their promising, with the Lord's assistance, to lead orderly lives in the future, they are again to be received into full communion with the church and to have the right hand of fellowship given them (Galatians 6:1; 2 Corinthians 2:7-8), but they are not on any account to be rebaptized (Ephesians 4:5).

CHAPTER IV. — *Of the Duties Incumbent on Church Members*

A church constituted after the heavenly pattern is as a city set on a hill, from which the glories of rich and free grace abundantly shine (Psalm 50:2). The true members of it have the light of the gospel shining in their hearts by the Holy Ghost and are entitled to all the blessings of the new covenant (Ephesians 1:3). Being thus blessed, their faith is a lively, active faith, not only purifying their hearts but working by love (Galatians 5:6), whereby they become the light of the world (Matthew 5:14-16), which they make apparent by a faithful discharge of the duties enjoined them by the Lord Jesus Christ, the great Head of the church (James 2:18).

1. As ministers are the representatives of Christ and employed by him in a work that is both useful and honorable, there are certain duties incumbent on all members of churches toward them.

(1) They owe them distinguishing honor and reverence, are to hold them in reputation as the ambassadors of Christ (Philippians 2:29; 2 Corinthians 5:20), and to esteem them highly for their work's sake (1 Thessalonians 5:13).

(2) They are to contribute according to their respective abilities toward their ministers' support (Galatians 6:6) that, being freed as much as possible from the cares of life, the ministers may wholly devote themselves to the duties of their holy function and have it in their power to use hospitality (1 Timothy 3:2) and stretch out the benevolent hand of charity to the poor in distress (Galatians 2:10), which maintenance ought not to be considered as a gratuity but as a debt due their minister. The law of nature requires it (1 Timothy 5:18). In the Lord's grants to Israel there was always a reserve made for the priests; under the gospel, provision is made for the support of the minister (1 Corinthians 9:7-14).

(3) They are to obey and submit themselves to their ministers (Ephesians 6:18-20).

(4) They ought to stand by and assist them in all their troubles and afflictions (2 Timothy 4:16; Job 6:14).

(5) They should receive no accusation against them without full proof (1 Timothy 5:19).

(6) Nor should they expose their infirmities (Acts 23:5; 3 John 10).

(7) They should follow their example, as far as they follow Christ (2 Thessalonians 3:7; 1 Corinthians 11:1).

2. Since deacons are in an honorable office in the church, the members are to respect and esteem them as being employed by the Lord to serve in the household of faith and as men whom, if faithful, God will greatly honor and bless (1 Timothy 3:13;

Matthew 25:21); to submit to their godly, and friendly admonitions (1 Corinthians 16:16); and to encourage them by cheerful and liberal contributions for the service of God's house, his ministers, and his poor (2 Corinthians 9:6-7).

3. The members of a church are bound in duty to love all men, but especially to love and do good to "them who are of the household of faith" (Galatians 6:10), and all must be done from a principle of love (1 John 4:7-11; John 13:34, 35). They are to "follow after the things which make for peace" (Romans 14:19), for they are to put the most favorable construction on words and actions that are doubtful (1 Corinthians 13:7), to speak no evil one of another (James 4:11), and to endeavor, by a disinterested and godly behavior, to sow the fruit of righteousness in peace (James 3:18), carefully avoiding whisperings and backbitings (2 Corinthians 12:20), not being busy meddlers with the concerns of others (2 Thessalonians 3:11); not taking up an evil report against another (Acts 25:16); nor doing anything "through strife or vainglory" (Philippians 2:3).

They are to pursue each other's edification and growth in grace (1 Thessalonians 5:11; 2 Peter 3:18); to pray for each other (James 5:16); and to visit each other, especially when sick or otherwise afflicted (Acts 15:36; James 1:27). Those visits ought to be improved for edification; therefore they should spend the time in praying together (Psalm 34:3); in godly conversation (Malachi 3:16); in exhorting and encouraging each other (Hebrews 3:13; Psalm 55:14); in warning and admonishing one another (1 Thessalonians 5:14; Romans 15:14); in ingenuously confessing their faults to one another, so far as Christian prudence will permit (James 5:16); and in administering all possible relief to the needy and distressed (James 2:15-16). As much as possible, they are to avoid going to law with each other (1 Corinthians 6:1-7); to prefer marrying among themselves, as far as it may be done with prudence (Amos 3:3; 2 Corinthians 6:14); and to labor to find out the cause of shyness in a brother, as soon as it is discovered (Matthew 5:23-24).

4. The duties of members to the church are as follows: to pray for its peace and prosperity and use their utmost endeavors to promote its welfare (Psalm 122:6-9); carefully to attend all church meetings, whether for public worship or business (Hebrews 10:25; Psalm 84:4,10); to submit to the order and discipline of the church, so far as it is consistent with the Word of God (Deuteronomy 5:1; Hebrews 13:17); to employ their talents and freely bestow of their substance for the service of the church (Romans 12:6-8; Proverbs 3:9,10); carefully to avoid jarrings, contentions, and quarrels in the church (1 Corinthians 10:32; Romans 2:8); and not to divulge any of the church's secrets (Song of Solomon 4:12).

CHAPTER V. — *Of Church Censures*

Rewards and penalties give sanction to law; therefore our Lord Jesus Christ, who is the only supreme Head of the church, in giving laws and institutions for the government thereof, has annexed rewards of grace to the faithful and obedient observers of them and punishments to be inflicted on the rebellious (Hebrews 11:6; Romans 2:6-9; Revelation 22:12).

There are some punishments which our righteous Lawgiver inflicts more immediately with his own hand, either by his providence in this world or by an infliction of divine wrath in the world to come. There are other punishments which Christ, by his Word, authorizes his church to inflict upon its rebellious and unworthy members. These are commonly called church censures, which differ in their nature according to the nature and degree of the offense and may be denominated rebuke, suspension, and excommunication.

1. Rebuke or admonition, the lowest degree of church censure, is reproving an offender, pointing out the offense, charging it upon the conscience, advising and exhorting him to repentance, watchfulness, and new obedience, and praying for him that he may be reclaimed (Titus 1:13). This, and all other church censures, must be administered in love and tenderness (Revelation 3:19); with Christian prudence (1 Timothy 1:2); in a sincere aim to save the soul from death (James 5:19-20; 2 Corinthians 13:10; Galatians 6:1); without partiality (1 Timothy 5:21); and as a caution to others (1 Timothy 5:20).

A member becomes worthy of rebuke (1) when, by the use of things in themselves indifferent, he wounds the conscience of a weak brother (1 Corinthians 8:11-12); (2) when he exposes to others the infirmities of a brother (1 Peter 4:8); (3) when he disquiets the peace of the brethren about matters of indifference (Romans 14:19-22); (4) when he, without a just cause, indulges anger against a brother (Matthew 5:22); (5) when he is contentious about unscriptural forms and fashions, as if they were necessary to be used in the church or among the members (1 Corinthians 11:16); (6) when he neglects privately to admonish or reprove a brother whom he knows to be guilty of sin (Leviticus 19:17); (7) when he neglects to attend church meetings for business (Acts 6:2); and (8) when he attends other places of worship to the neglect of his own (Hebrews 10:25).

2. Suspension, considered as a church censure, is that act of a church whereby an offending member, being found guilty, is set aside from office, from the Lord's table, and from the liberty of judging or voting in any case. By this act the staff beauty is broken, but not the staff bands (Zechariah 11:10,14). Since this censure does not cut off from union, but only from communion with the church, the suspended member is not to be accounted an enemy, but admonished as a brother (2 Thessalonians 3:15), and upon a credible profession of repentance the censure is to be taken off and the delinquent restored to all the privileges of the church.

This censure is to be administered in case of crimes which do not amount so high as to deserve excommunication, as (1) when a member breaks the peace of the church by janglings and disputings (1 Timothy 1:6; 6:5); (2) when he withdraws from the church on account of its wholesome discipline, notwithstanding loving admonitions given him (John 6:66; Jude 19); (3) when he leaves his place at the Lord's table for the sake of another member with whom he is offended and neglects to do his duty by him as directed (Matthew 18:15); (4) when he broaches unsound, heretical principles (Titus 3:10); (5) when he is a busy tattler and backbiter (Psalm 50:19-21); (6) when he through sloth neglects the necessary duties of life (1 Timothy 5:8); (7) when he has committed a gross crime but gives some tokens of repentance, he is to be suspended that the church may have time to judge of his sincerity (1 John 4:1); (8) when a party of members, like Korah and his company,[130] break through their covenant obligations and attempt to set up for themselves, in an irregular manner and in opposition to all the loving persuasions of the majority, being "trucebreakers" and "despisers of those that are good" (2 Timothy 3:3). In a word, all practices that in their own nature and tendency are destructive of the reputation, peace, and prosperity of the church and yet appear not to be past remedy merit this censure.

3. As excommunication is on all hands acknowledged to be an ordinance of Christ, the great Head of the church, and a censure in its own nature, very important, awful, and tremendous, it is highly needful that churches should well understand the nature of it.

Excommunication is a censure of the highest degree; it is a judicial act of the church in which, by the authority of Christ, she cuts off and entirely excludes an unworthy member from union and communion with the church and from all the rights and privileges thereof. "It is a disfranchising from all the immunities of a fellow-citizen with the saints, and taking from him a place and a name in the house of God."[131]

This censure, awful as it is, respects only the spiritual concerns of a man, as related to the church, and does by no means affect his temporal estate or civil affairs; it does not subject him to fines, imprisonment, or death; it does not interfere with the

---

[130] Numbers 16.

[131] Gill, *Body of Divinity*, III, 285.

business of the civil magistrate; nor does it break in upon the natural and civil relations between man and wife, parents and children, masters and servants; nor does it forbid attendance on the external ministry of the Word.

"To deliver" an offender "unto Satan for the destruction of the flesh" (1 Corinthians 5:5) was an act purely apostolical, for it was not the act of the church.

> Nor is this a form of excommunication; nor was this phrase ever used in excommunicating persons by the primitive churches; nor ought it ever to be used; it is what no man or set of men have power to do now, since the ceasing of the extraordinary gifts of the Spirit, which the apostles were endowed with, who, as they had a power over Satan to dispossess him from the bodies of men, so to deliver up the bodies of men into his hands.[132]

Hence the Apostle, writing to Timothy on a similar case, expresses it as done by himself, not by the church (1 Timothy 1:20).

The act of excommunication is expressed by various phrases, as, by avoiding similar conversation with such (Romans 16:17); by not keeping company with them (1 Corinthians 5:9; Ephesians 5:11); by not eating with them at the Lord's table (1 Corinthians 5:11); by purging out from them the old leaven (1 Corinthians 5:7); by putting away the wicked from among them (1 Corinthians 5:13); by withdrawing from disorderly persons and by cutting them off from fellowship with them (2 Thessalonians 3:6; Galatians 5:12).

The subjects of this ordinance are members who are guilty of some notorious and atrocious crimes, which are so, either in their own nature or by means of sundry aggravations. There are some crimes so high and pernicious in their own nature as to call for a speedy excommunication, unless the most evident

---

[132] Gill, *Exposition*, II, 178.

marks of repentance appear in the offender, as (1) all sins that are against the letter of the Ten Commandments (Romans 7:12; Matthew 5:17); (2) all that call for severe corporal punishment from human laws, provided those laws are not contrary to the laws of God (Proverbs 8:15; Romans 13:1-4; 1 Peter 2:13-14); and (3) all such sins as are highly scandalous in their nature and expose the church to contempt (1 Timothy 5:24; 1 Corinthians 5:2). We find black catalogs of sins which call for this censure (1 Corinthians 5:11; 6:9-10). Indeed for crimes of an inferior nature, when aggravated by a contumacious despising of the authority of the church and after the more gentle censures have been used, excommunication ought to take place.

But an offender, even of the highest rank, who gives clear, evident, and satisfactory proofs of a true, sincere, evangelical repentance is by no means to be excommunicated. Does not reason itself suggest that we ought to forgive those who repent and those whom God has forgiven? Christ our great pattern did so, as appears in the case of the woman taken in adultery (John 8:11). Peter also is an instance of Christ's readiness to forgive penitents. Peter was a member of that congregation in the midst of which Christ sang praises to his Father (Psalm 22:22). Peter fell foully; he denied his Master with oaths and curses — a horrid crime! Did Christ immediately cut him off? No, but admonished him by a look; the offender repented; the penitent was forgiven. Let churches follow the example which Christ has set for them.

The act of excommunication may not be performed by a member on himself; such a one, says Dr. Gill, is *a felo de se*;[133] he is, in effect, a self-murderer. As consent is necessary to a person's coming into the church, so none can go out of it without its consent. To attempt it is to break the covenant with the church, and, as much as in a man lies, to break up the church. By the same rule that one member may thus leave the

---

[133] I.e., one who commits suicide or dies as the result of wilfully committing an unlawful act, *Body of Divinity*, III, 2, 286.

church, another may, the pastor may, all may. The tendency of this conduct, as all may see, is confusion and destruction. Those therefore who are guilty of it ought to be looked upon as trucebreakers — proud, arrogant, dangerous persons — and to be dealt with as such. They should be avoided by all other churches.

No man has a right of himself to perform this censure; it is a punishment inflicted by many (2 Corinthians 2:6). But this great censure is to be executed

> by the elders (ministers) of churches, with the consent of the members of them; for they have a right to do this, previous to their having elders, and when they have none, as to receive members, so to expel them. The power of it originally lies in the church; the authority of executing it lies in the elders with the consent and by the order of the church, as the directions to the churches concerning this matter testify.[134]

To proceed regularly in this solemn business, the church must cite an accused member to appear, either at a stated church meeting of business, or at an occasional meeting for that purpose in order that he may have a fair trial and an opportunity of making his defense, if he has any to make. The meeting is opened by prayer for direction. Then the case is impartially examined and tried by the Word of God. If the accused member is found guilty of a crime deserving excommunication, he is not to be cut off immediately, unless it be some extraordinary case, but admonished, and given some time for repentance and for the church to mourn over him and pray for him. If the offender continues obstinate and appears to be incorrigible, the church is under a necessity of proceeding to the execution of the great censure against him.

If the offense be private the censure may, and in some cases ought to, be laid on before the church only;[135] but if the crime is

---

[134] *Ibid.*, III, 287.

[135] I.e., should be made public to and considered only by the church.

censure to be public (1 Timothy 5:20; Jude 22). In this case the church appoints the day and summons the guilty member to attend. The minister suits his sermon to the occasion, after which he prays to God for a blessing on the ordinance to be administered. Then he proceeds to sum up the sentence of the church; he lays open the odious nature of the crime and the dreadful load of guilt which the sin, with its aggravations, has brought upon the offender; he takes notice of the scandal it has brought upon religion; the dishonor it has brought to God and the grief it has brought to the church; he observes that the excommunicating act is not intended for the destruction of the soul but is used as a last remedy for the recovery of the offender and as a caution to others. Then, by the authority of the Lord Jesus Christ and in the name and behalf of that church, he cuts off and secludes the offender by name from union and communion with the church. Since he has broken his covenant with them, they also break their covenant with him, praying the Lord Jesus Christ, who is the Good Shepherd, to restore him by giving him unfeigned repentance that he may again be received into the sheepfold.

If the accused member should obstinately refuse to appear before the church, when cited as above, it is to be deemed a sign of guilt, a contempt of the authority of the church, and an aggravation of his crime; and the process of the church against him shall not be obstructed on account of his absence.

If it should happen that the minister of the church is the offender or that the church is without a minister, they[136] ought, in either of these cases, to call one from a sister church to assist them on such an occasion; for, as has been before observed, the authority of executing this censure, as well as all other ordinances in general, lies in the elders.

The ends to be answered by this solemn ordinance, which should always be aimed at in its administration, are as follows.

---

[136] I.e., the members.

The glory of God is the ultimate end, for as his name is dishonored by the evil practices or principles of church members, so this is the most open and most effectual way of removing the dishonor that is brought upon it.

Another end is the purging of the church and the preserving of it from infection. "A little leaven leavens the whole lump" and therefore "the old leaven" must be purged out, that the church may become "a new lump." "Evil communications corrupt good manners,"[137] and therefore evil men must be put away from among the saints (1 Corinthians 5:6-7,13). Lepers were to be put out of the camp that they might not infect others; and erroneous persons, whose words do eat as a canker,[138] must be removed from the communion of churches.

A church of Christ is like a garden or vineyard, which, if not taken care of and this ordinance of excommunication not used, will be like the vineyard of the slothful, overrun with thorns, nettles, and other weeds; but by means of this it is cleared of the weeds of immoralities and the bitter roots of false doctrines are plucked up and eradicated, and withered branches are gathered and cast out.

The good of persons excommunicated is another end and is sometimes effected by it. God blesses his own institution when rightly performed; i.e., for edification and not destruction, for the saving of the souls of men who are hereby brought to shame and repentance for their sins, at which time they are to be received again with all love and tenderness and to be comforted, that they may not be "swallowed up with overmuch sorrow" (Jude 23; 2 Thessalonians 3:14; 2 Corinthians 2:7).

---

[137] Cf. 1 Corinthians 15:33.

[138] Cf. 2 Timothy 2:17.

CHAPTER VI. — *Of the Association of Churches*

As the communion of saints, so the communion of churches is a desirable blessing. To obtain and promote such ought to be the study and endeavor of all the people of God.

Although churches formed on the gospel plan are independent of each other with regard to power, yet not so, strictly speaking, with regard to communion. For as saints in general have an indisputable right to share in each other's gifts and graces, so have churches in this joint capacity. The general rule "to do good and to communicate forget not" (Hebrews 13:16) is applicable in a particular manner to churches as such.

In order the more amply to obtain this blessing of communion, there ought to be a coalescing or uniting of several churches into one body, so far as their local situation and other circumstances will admit. But as it is impracticable for all the individual members thus to associate and coalesce together, the churches should each respectively choose and delegate some of the most able, pious, and judicious from among themselves, and particularly their ministers, to convene at such times and places as may be thought most conducive to the great end proposed and to act as their representatives in the general assembly. Their expenses ought to be defrayed by the churches that send them.

These delegates, at their first meeting, are in a formal manner to enter into covenant with each other, as the representatives of the churches, for the promoting of Christ's cause in general and for the interest of the churches they represent in particular. They should then form their plan of operation and decide on the most proper time and place for meeting in the future. Once a year at least they ought to meet at the place most central and convenient for all the churches in conferment to attend.

Although such a conjunction of churches is not expressly commanded in the Scriptures, yet it receives sufficient countenance and authority from the light of nature and the general laws of society, but more especially from a precedent established by apostolic authority (Acts 15).

The association thus formed is a respectable body, as it represents not a city, country, or nation, but the churches of Jesus Christ. Yet it is by no means to be deemed a superior judicature vested with coercive power or authority over the churches; it presumes not to impose its sentiments upon its constituents, under pain of excommunication. Nor does it anathematize those who do not implicitly submit to its determinations, which would be nothing less than spiritual tyranny and better comport with[139] the arbitrary spirit of popish councils than with that meekness which distinguishes the true disciples and humble followers of the lowly yet adorable Jesus. The apostles, elders, and brethren who composed the first Christian council presumed not to impose their conclusions upon the churches in such a lordly manner but prefaced their determinations with this modest prologue, "It seemed good to the Holy Ghost, and to us, to lay upon you no greater burden than these necessary things" (Acts 15:28). The Baptist association therefore arrogates no higher title than that of an advisory council. Consistent with this epithet, it ought ever to act, when it acts at all, without intruding on the rights of independent congregational churches or usurping authority over them (Matthew 23:10-12).

Nevertheless, the association has a natural and unalienable right to judge for itself which churches shall be admitted into confederacy with it and to withdraw from all acts of communion and fellowship with any church, so admitted, provided such church should obstinately persist in holding corrupt principles or indulging vicious practices, notwithstanding[140] all proper endeavors have been used to reclaim it (Ephesians 5:7; Revelation 18:4).

---

[139] I.e., correspond to.

[140] I.e., although.

An association, when transacting business, should proceed in the following manner: (1) Always begin and end each session by prayer. (2) Admit none as messengers but such as come recommended by letters, well authenticated, from the churches to which they belong or from whence they come. (3) When a church petitions by letter for admission, if approved of, the moderator is to inform the messengers that their request is granted and invite[141] them to take their seats. (4) All who have anything to offer are to rise and address the moderator. (5) While one is speaking, the rest are to be silent; yet all have an equal right to speak in turn. (6) No partiality or respect of persons is to be shown. (7) Every matter should be canvassed[142] with gravity, modesty, and a sincere aim after truth. (8) When all are not agreed, the matter may be put to a vote, and a majority determines. (9) All queries regularly sent by the churches should be answered, if possible. (10) Any matter proposed, relative to the general good of the churches, should be seriously attended to. (11) Every transaction should be conformable to the revealed will of God. (12) A circular letter should be written and sent to all the churches in confederation, containing such instruction, information, and advice as may be thought most suitable. With such should be sent the transactions of the association.

The benefits arising from an association and communion of churches are many. In general, it will tend toward maintaining the truth, order, and discipline of the gospel.

By it the churches may have such doubts as arise amongst them cleared, and this will prevent disputes (Acts 15:28-29).

They will be furnished with salutary counsel (Proverbs 11:14).

Those churches which have no ministers may obtain occasional supplies (Song of Solomon 8:8).

---

[141] The original uses here "desire" in its now obsolete usage "invite."

[142] I.e., considered.

The churches will be more closely united in promoting the cause and interest of Christ.

A member who is aggrieved through partiality or any other wrong received from the church may have an opportunity of applying for direction.

A godly and sound ministry will be encouraged, while a ministry that is unsound and ungodly will be discountenanced.

There will be a reciprocal communication of their gifts (Philippians 4:15).

Ministers may alternately be sent out to preach the gospel to those who are destitute (Galatians 2:9).

A large party may draw off from the church by means of an intruding minister, or other ways, and the aggrieved may have no way of obtaining redress but from the association.

A church may become heretical, so that with it its godly members can no longer communicate, yet it can obtain no relief but by the association.

Contentions may arise between sister churches, which the association is most likely to remove.

The churches may have candidates for the ministry properly tried by the association.

These and other advantages arising from an association must induce every godly church to desire a union with such a body. But should any stand off, it would argue much self-sufficiency (Revelation 3:17) and little or no desire after the unity of the Spirit (Ephesians 4:3) or mutual edification (1 Corinthians 12:11-14).

ABOUT THE AUTHOR

James Leo Garrett, Jr.

James Leo Garrett, Jr., is Distinguished Professor of Theology, Emeritus, at Southwestern Baptist Theological Seminary in Fort Worth, Texas. He holds a B.A. from Baylor University, a B.D. and a Th.D. from Southwestern Baptist Seminary, a Th.M. from Princeton Theological Seminary, and a Ph.D. from Harvard University. He has also studied at the Catholic University of America, the University of Oxford, St. John's University, and Trinity Evangelical Divinity School. He was professor of Christian theology at Southern Baptist Theological Seminary, Louisville, Kentucky, and was director of the J. M. Dawson Studies in Church and State, the Simon M. and Ethel Bunn Professor of Church-State Studies, and professor of religion at Baylor University. In Hong Kong Baptist Theological Seminary he was visiting professor.

Garrett has been author, co-author, editor, or co-editor, of a dozen books, including *The Concept of the Believers' Church* (Herald Press, 1970), *Baptist Relations with Other Christians* (Judson Press, 1974), and *Are Southern Baptists "Evangelicals"?* (Mercer University Press, 1983). He has contributed chapters to twenty-one other books and was refounding managing editor of *Southwestern Journal of Theology* and editor of *Journal of Church and State*.

A pastor or interim pastor of a number of Baptist churches, he also served as coordinator of the first Conference on the Concept of the Believers' Church, as chairman of the Commission on Cooperative Christianity of the Baptist World Alliance, as a participant in Roman Catholic-Southern Baptist dialogues and Baptist World Alliance-Eastern Orthodox pre-conversations, and was recently co-chairman of the Division of Study and Research of the Baptist World Alliance.

Professor Garrett has three sons and lives with his wife, Myrta Ann, in Fort Worth.

THE BAPTIST STANDARD BEARER, INC.
A non-profit, tax-exempt corporation
committed to the Publication and Preservation
of The Baptist Heritage.

**SAMPLE TITLES FOR PUBLICATIONS AVAILABLE
IN OUR VARIOUS SERIES:**

THE BAPTIST *COMMENTARY* SERIES
Sample of authors/works in or near production:
John Gill - *Exposition of the Old & New Testaments (9 Vol. Set)*
John Gill - *Exposition of Solomon's Song*

THE BAPTIST *FAITH* SERIES:
Sample of authors/works in or near production:
Abraham Booth - *The Reign of Grace*
John Fawcett - *Christ Precious to Those That Believe*
John Gill - *A Complete Body of Doctrinal & Practical Divinity (2 Vols.)*

THE BAPTIST *HISTORY* SERIES:
Sample of authors/works in or near production:
Thomas Armitage - *A History of the Baptists (2 Vols.)*
Isaac Backus - *History of the New England Baptists (2 Vols.)*
William Cathcart - *The Baptist Encyclopaedia (3 Vols.)*
J. M. Cramp - *Baptist History*

THE BAPTIST *DISTINCTIVES* SERIES:
Sample of authors/works in or near production:
Abraham Booth - *Paedobaptism Examined (3 Vols.)*
Alexander Carson - *Ecclesiastical Polity of the New Testament Churches*
E. C. Dargan - *Ecclesiology: A Study of the Churches*
J. M. Frost - *Pedobaptism: Is It From Heaven?*
R. B. C. Howell - *The Evils of Infant Baptism*

THE *DISSENT & NONCONFORMITY* SERIES:
Sample of authors/works in or near production:
Champlin Burrage - *The Early English Dissenters (2 Vols.)*
Albert H. Newman - *History of Anti-Pedobaptism*
Walter Wilson - *The History & Antiquities of the Dissenting Churches (4 Vols.)*

For a complete list of current authors/titles, visit our internet site at
www.standardbearer.org or write us at:

The Baptist Standard Bearer, Inc.
No. 1 Iron Oaks Drive • Paris, Arkansas 72855

Telephone: (479)-963-3831   Fax: (479)-963-8083
E-mail: baptist@arkansas.net
Internet: http://www.standardbearer.org

Thou hast given a *standard* to them that fear thee; that it may be displayed because of the truth. -- Psalm 60:4

www.ingramcontent.com/pod-product-compliance
Lightning Source LLC
LaVergne TN
LVHW091316080426
835510LV00007B/517